BIBLICAL INSIGHTS
AND
SPECIAL THOUGHTS

READINGS TO WEIGH AND CONSIDER

DAVID L. LEATHERMAN

TABLE OF CONTENTS

Chapter 3 – Mission Trips

ACKNOWLEDGMENTS

My first acknowledgment is to my God who, I believe, revealed His truth and allowed my hand to put it in writing. Studying God's Word to understand His knowledge and His wisdom has been a hoppy of mine. Because of my curiosity and analytical mind, I would take various topics from the Bible and study them in great detail. After the study was completed, a report was written, outlining the results of the study. Many of these writings were then handed out to various people, including ministers. Their reactions were very positive. And, so, the idea for this book developed. This is the second book He has published by my hand in writing. The first book is entitled <u>Something to Consider</u>.

The second acknowledgment is to my wife, Dorinda, who was so vital to the publishing of my first book. She encouraged me to write a second book. She went beyond encouragement and became my editor as well as critic. She has put many hours in typing, editing and analyzing these writings. For all that she has done to enable me to publish this book, I want to give a special acknowledgment of thanks.

Last, but no less important, I want to acknowledge Mark Dearman, Interim Children's Minister at my church, Hope Church of Tupelo, MS. Mark very graciously agreed to proofread my manuscript. I want to thank Mark for his time and effort in undergoing this proofreading.

PREFACE

I t is strange how this book got started. My mind is an engineering and analytical mind; my quest for knowledge and wisdom is sometimes overpowering. The question: Who can be a blessing and a curse? When God came into my life and revealed Himself to me, I wanted to know who is this man Jesus. If I was going to give myself to Him, I wanted to know whom I was giving myself to, and a reason why I should give up myself to Him. So, the pursuit began. WOW—what a journey I have had in this pursuit from that time on.

I studied God's Word, the Bible, with objective mind. The more I studied, the more He revealed to me. Proverbs Chapter 2 essentially says to pursue God as though He is the most valuable treasure on earth. Then, He will first teach you to fear Him (reverence Him), and then He will reveal His knowledge and wisdom to you. WOW! That has been so true. What I have found is this: God is not going to be in competition with the TV or cellphone or any other device. Jesus said to knock and He will reveal Himself to you. If I pursue Him first, He will be with me. He is not going to share His time with me.

The first book He wrote, Something to Consider, was inspired in our quiet time together in a deer stand. If you are a deer hunter, you know that you have a lot of quiet. I often thought I had to solve the world's problems during the quiet times.

Now, regarding this book—each day I would have my "you and me God" quiet time. It was a great time, but no great revelations. Then, there were those times when an event or scripture would come to my mind, and God would pour out His knowledge and wisdom about those scriptures and events. I would grab a pen and paper, and His message would flow through my hand into these writings. After it was finished, I would read it and realize what was given was beyond my abilities of knowledge and wisdom. I would share these with people through email and personal handouts. There was large feedback on how helpful they were and how they impacted their lives. Based on that, I was encouraged to put the writings in a book form.

Part of my testimony is what I have referred to as "Our Calling and Our Footprints".

OUR CALLING AND OUR FOOTPRINTS

In our beginning, our birth, God breathed life into a perfectly formed handful of dust. When He breathed life into that handful of dust, He also breathed an eternally living spirit, and then gave the body a spirit and a commission, or purpose, to serve Him. Everybody is created for a purpose, commonly said to be a "calling". What is yours?

I think I know my calling—when I gave my life to Jesus, it was a transformation to one of the many revelations He gave to me. He gave me a calling for the souls of the lost and to minister to what society calls "the least of these". I felt a calling to the mission field, which at that time I thought was to go to impoverished places and countries. Later, I discovered that my calling and mission field was here with my own family and community. I never lost a desire and an overwhelming need to go to all parts of the world to fulfill the Great Commission. I can feel the pain of hunger and agony of the downtrodden. I can hear the cries of those who are in hell, because they did not receive the saving grace of the blood of Jesus. Because of this passion in my heart for "the least of these" and the "lost souls", I have committed my life to what I feel my calling is.

When I gave my life to Christ, I had no idea He would take me down the path that he has. It has been an exciting journey. He has allowed me to minister to victims here in the U.S.A., like victims of hurricane Katrina, victims of a tornado in Smithville, Ms, and especially people of the community I live in. He has also allowed, or called, me to represent him in many countries, like England (3 times), Wales, Germany (3 times), Switzerland, Liechtenstein, France (3 times), Austria, Italy (3 times), Greece, Bulgaria, Venice, Crete, Israel (3 times), Turkey, Jordan (2 times) Syria, South Korea, Japan, The Philippines (11 times), Buenos Aires, Argentina, Mexico (many times), United Arab Emeritus, Honduras (5 times), Belize, Nepal, Ecuador, Canada, India, Cuba (2) , Bahamas (2 times), South Africa, Malawi Africa, Mozambique Africa, Spain, China and other countries.

Question: Why am I keeping track of this history? Well, everybody leaves footprints in the sands of their life. Hopefully, my footprints are pleasing to God, even though there are footprints that I regret and am ashamed of. God loves you and can use your footprints!

My mission model is Luke 4:18,19:

> "The Spirit of the Lord is on me, because he has anointed me to preach good news to the poor. He has sent me to proclaim freedom for the prisoners and recovery of sight for the blind, to release the oppressed, to proclaim the year of the Lord's favor".

My prayer is Ephesians 6:19:

> "Pray also for me, that whenever I open my mouth, words may be given me so that I will

fearlessly make known the mystery of the gospel, for which I am an ambassador in chains. Pray that I may declare it fearlessly, as I should".

My life's goal and motto - Psalm 119:33-37:

"Teach me, O Lord, to follow your decrees; then I will keep them to the end. Give me understanding, and I will keep your law and obey it with all my heart. Direct me in the path of your commands, for there I find delight. Turn my heart toward your statutes and not toward selfish gain. Turn my eyes away from worthless things; preserve my life according to your word".

My commission – Ephesians 3:8-11

"Although I am less than the least of all God's people, this grace was given to me; to preach to the Gentiles the unsearchable riches of Christ and to make plain to everyone the administration of this mystery, which for ages past was kept hidden in God, who created all things. His intent was that now, through the church, the manifold wisdom of God should be made known to the rulers and authorities in the heavenly realms, according to his eternal purpose which he accomplished in Christ Jesus our Lord."

I hope you enjoy reading this book as much as I have enjoyed working with my Father to prepare it.

CHAPTER 1

INSIGHTS INTO SPIRITUAL THINGS

A PRAYER TO THE TRIUNE GOD

F ATHER, You are my fortress and my sure defense. You are my rock of refuge, my high tower, my shield and my buckler. You are my righteousness and the strength of my life. You are my light and salvation; therefore, I have nothing to fear. You are my Creator and Sustainer. In my mother's womb You formed me. I am fearfully and wonderfully made by You. Thank You for calling me to be your child.

LORD JESUS, You are my Shepherd; I shall not want. You are the Word of Life. You are Emmanuel, God with us. You are the One who shows me my Heavenly Father. I thank You that You are the First and the Last, the Alpha and the Omega. You are the Son of Righteousness, the Rose of Sharon. You are the Fairest of Ten Thousand. You are the Lily of the Valley, the Bright and Morning Star. You are called the Wonderful Counselor, the Mighty God, the Everlasting Father and the Prince of Peace. At Your name, every knee will bow and every tongue will confess that You are Lord, to the glory of God. You are the God in whom I live and move and have my being. Thank You for dying for me.

HOLY SPIRIT, You are my Comforter, my Teacher and my Helper. You live within me and come along side me to help me become more like Jesus. You convict me of sin, righteousness and judgment. You fill me with Your fullness when I ask. Thank You for molding me into the image of Jesus.

Thank you, Triune God, for being all that I will ever need. Amen

(Author Unknown)

A TREE AND ITS FRUITS

Matthew 7:15-23

"Watch out for false prophets. They come to you in sheep's clothing, but inwardly they are ferocious wolves. By their fruits you will recognize them. Do people pick grapes from thorn bushes, or figs from thistles? Likewise, every good tree bears good fruit, but a bad tree bears bad fruit. A good tree cannot bear bad fruit, and a bad tree cannot bear good fruit. Every tree that does not bear good fruit is cut down and thrown into the fire. Thus, by their fruit you will recognize them. Not everyone who says to me, 'Lord, Lord' will enter the kingdom of heaven, but only he who does the will of my Father who is in heaven. Many will say to me on that day, 'Lord, Lord, did we not prophesy in your name, and in your name drive out demons and perform many miracles?' Then I will tell them plainly, 'I never knew you. Away from me, you evildoers!'"

In the course of my college education, I ran across an inscription posted at the top of the college library entrance that read, "Read not to believe or take for granted, nor to refute or contradict, but to weigh and consider". That inscription has had a huge impact on my life. I try to embrace that attitude when I read, listen and observe. A similar attitude shows up in the book of Thessalonians. A directive was issued to the Christians in Paul's letter to the Thessalonians when he admonishes them to test all things to the scriptures so that you will not be led astray.

Again, Matthew 7:15 says "Watch out for false prophets. They will come to you in sheep's clothing, but inwardly they are ferocious wolves." Verse 16 says, "By their fruits you will recognize them." Scripture says that the wolves will come in sheep's clothing. The wolves can be ever so clever. They will wear the sheep's clothing of doing good deeds and intentions for the cause of something good or for the cause of Christ, but beneath it all, their true intensions or desires are to do something that will serve their best interests. And that is the deal killer for Jesus. The false prophet can wear the cloak of religiosity and represent itself in the form of a person, preacher, teacher, church, missionary, evangelist, and many other ways. Here is the rule that will test a false prophet in my judgment. If a person or entity is acting on behalf of God and only God's standards of righteousness and serves to glorify God, then he/she is a true prophet for the purpose of God. If, on the other hand, he/she has any self-serving motive, like pride, prestige, power or possessions, then he/she becomes a false prophet that dilutes God's purpose and leads many astray. The scripture says cursed are those who lead one astray.

Verse 16 says, "By the fruits you will recognize them". All fruit comes from a nourishing source like a tree, vine, etc. Verses 17,18. Good fruit comes from good nourishment (like God's truth), but bad fruit comes from deception, which is anything other than God's truth. Bad fruit leads to bad things.

Verse 19 says, 'Every tree that does not bear good fruit is cut down and thrown into the fire'. Jesus is saying to get out into the world and bear good fruit, fruit that will truly represent His plan and purpose. If the tree does not get out into the world and does not bear good fruit, it will be cut down and thrown into the fire.

Verses 21-23 says "Not everyone who says to me, 'Lord, Lord'' will enter the kingdom of heaven, but only he who does the will of my Father who is in heaven. Many will say to me on that day, 'Lord, Lord, did we not prophesy in your name and in your name drive out demons and perform many miracles'? Then I will tell them plainly, 'I never knew you. Away from me, you evil doers'. These scriptures are self evident. If you were a false prophet and stood before Jesus He would say, "I never knew you. Away from me you evil doer". Jesus is the only way into heaven. Not knowing Jesus is the only way into hell which is eternal damnation of suffering and pain.

Remember, the standards that determine eternal judgment are not a person's standards, not a church's standard, not a preacher's standard, but <u>only</u> God's standards set forth in His Bible. We are responsible for our own choices.

A WARNING AGAINST UNFAITHFULNESS AND/OR FALLING AWAY FROM THE LORD

Who is saved and who is not saved among those who call themselves a Christian? That is a question that is a very daunting fact. Jesus talked directly and indirectly about that subject. If a person is saved, what is next and what must be done. Those are questions and a subject that volumes of thoughts have been written on. Following is a brief discussion of a very narrow perspective that might be something to consider. First, let us review the scriptures; then let us analyze these scriptures to see how God describes an expectation of what He desires from us, to be qualified as a follower of Him.

The scriptures are clear about who is a true Christian and those who have the illusion of being a Christian. The scriptures first, then the analysis.

In the book of Hebrews, chapter 5:7-14 begins a message that continues through Hebrews 6:1-12:

> Hebrews 5:7-14 - 7) "During the days of Jesus' life on earth, he offered up prayers and petitions with loud cries and tears to the one who could save him from death, and he was heard because of his reverent submission. 8) Although he was a son, he learned obedience from what he suffered 9)and once made perfect, he became the source of eternal salvation for all who obey him 10) and was designated by God to be high priest in the order of Melchizedek. 11) We have much to say about this, but it is hard to explain because you are slow to learn. 12) In fact, though by this time you ought to be teachers, you need someone to teach you the elementary truths of God's word all over again. You need milk, not solid food! 13) Anyone who lives on milk, being still an infant, is not acquainted with the teaching about righteousness. 14) But solid food is for the mature, which by constant use have trained themselves to distinguish good from evil."

> Hebrews 6:1-12 - 1) Therefore let us leave the elementary teachings about Christ and go on to maturity, not laying again the foundation of repentance from acts that lead to death and of faith in God, 2) instruction about baptisms, the laying on of hands, the resurrection of the dead, and eternal judgment. 3) And God permitting,

we will do so.4) It is impossible for those who have once been enlightened, who have tasted the heavenly gift, who have shared in the Holy Spirit, 5)who have tasted the goodness of the word of God and the powers of the coming age, 6) if they fall away, to be brought back to repentance, because to their loss, they are crucifying the Son of God all over again and subjecting him to public disgrace. 7) Land that drinks in the rain often falling on it and produces a crop useful to those for whom it is farmed receives the blessing of God. 8) But land that produces thorns and thistles is worthless and is in danger of being cursed. In the end it will be burned. 9) Even though we speak like this, dear friends, we are confident of better things in your case – things that accompany salvation. 10) God is not unjust; he will not forget your work and the love you have shown him as you have helped his people and continue to help them. 11) We want each of you to show this same diligence to the very end, in order to make your hope sure. 12) We do not want you to become lazy, but to imitate those, who through faith and patience inherit what has been promised.

THE ANALYSIS

Chapter 5:7-10 – verse 9 declares him "the source of eternal salvation". There is no method or church or spiritual leader or religious practice, no baptism or speaking in tongues, or church attendance, or tithing, or singing in the choir, or anything that will be a source to eternal salvation; only the blood of Jesus as is revealed in Hebrews chapter nine – Only Jesus, plus nothing else!

Chapter 5:11-14 – Read it again. Jesus wants followers who want to desire a relationship with Him – a deep and meaningful relationship with Him. Yet, so many self-proclaimed Christians do not pursue Him. At some point in their life, they have had an emotional experience and made a proclamation of believing in Jesus, but have never taken an interest and have no desire to know who He is. They are content with that initial emotional experience and are interested in going to church or chasing emotional experiences to support this shallow sense of religiosity. The scripture refers this relationship as baby's milk, rather than the solid food of studying and knowing and doing God's standard of righteousness that was given to us as the last known truth given to man, which is the Holy Bible.

Chapter 6:1-3 – "Therefore, let us leave the elementary teachings about Christ and go on to maturity, not laying again the foundation of repentance from acts that lead to death, and of faith in God, instruction about baptisms, the laying on of hands, the resurrection of the dead, and eternal judgment. And God permitting, we will do so".

This scripture is telling us to move beyond the elementary teaching about Christ. Those teachings should already be in the heart of a mature believer. There are so many "Christians" that go to church week after week and go from one bible study to another bible study and never move beyond this elementary process to experience the true passion of Jesus Christ by actually <u>doing</u> the will of Jesus. So often, this process has become a very selfish and self-serving act to satisfy an internal need to fulfill a sense of spirituality. It serves self rather than God. Hebrews 8:10 says that God put within us his laws in our minds and wrote them in our hearts. NOTE: I want to make something very clear. Going from bible study to bible study, or from church to church, is a <u>good</u> thing <u>if</u> you allow these experiences to draw you to a more intimate relationship with God that results in a desire to <u>apply</u> what you learn. In other words, to gain "heart" knowledge and not just "head" knowledge.

19

Chapter 6:4-6 – "It is impossible for those who have once been enlightened, who have tasted the heavenly gift, who have shared in the Holy spirit, who have tasted the goodness of the word of God and the powers of the coming age, if they fall away, to be brought back to repentance, because to their loss, they are crucifying the Son of God all over again and subjecting him to public disgrace."

This is interesting. The scripture refers to those "who have tasted the heavenly gift", who have "shared in the Holy Spirit", "who have tasted the goodness of the word of God". The word "tasted" has a specific meaning. To taste something means to not internalize or not to fully consume all there is to consume. Jesus does not want us to taste who he really is, but, rather to consume fully all that he fully is.

Now for verse 6: "if they fall away, to be brought back to repentance, because to their loss, they are crucifying the Son of God all over again, and subjecting him to public disgrace."

The scripture says that if a "Christian" continues to fall away from God, by choosing to willfully sin, that "Christian" causes Jesus to constantly be crucified again and again and subjects him to a public disgrace. Wow! That is something a "Christian" needs to understand and focus on. How many times do we send Him back to the cross?

Chapter 6:7,8 – "Land that drinks in the rain often falling on it and that produces a crop useful to those for which it was farmed receives the blessing of God. But land that produces thorns and thistles is worthless and is in danger of being cursed. In the end, it will be burned."

This appears to be a warning. If a "Christian's" land, which represents the works of his life, produces thorns and thistles, it is worthless to him and is in danger of being consumed in fire. Wow. Think about that! Also consider Matthew 25:45,46. (Jesus was discussing how we must take care of the least of the people). "He will reply, 'I tell you the truth. Whatever you did not do for one of the least of these, you did not do for me.

Then they will go away to eternal punishment, but the righteous to eternal life." It does not sound like a good situation to me. A "Christian" who does not do God's work can be thrown into eternal punishment.

Chapter 6:9-12 – "Even though we speak like this, dear friends, we are confident of better things in your case – things that accompany salvation. God is not unjust; he will not forget your work and the love you have shown him as you have helped his people and continue to help them. We want each of you to show this same diligence to the very end, <u>in order to make your hope sure</u>. <u>We do not want you to become lazy</u>, but to imitate those who through faith and patience inherit what has been promised."

I love these verses, because it says "God is not unjust". Which means He is just. Actually, God defines who being "just" is. Then he defines that statement by saying "he will not forget your work and the love you have shown him as you have helped his people and continue to help them." Did you catch that: You show love to Jesus by showing mercy and by helping others. Wow.

Then there is verse 12:"We do not want you to become lazy, but to imitate those who through faith and patience inherit what has been promised."

These scriptures speak the heart of Jesus and the mission we have in our relationship with Jesus as we serve Him. Do not be lazy in our works and passion to serve Him. Here is something else to consider: Jesus was praying His most passionate prayer to His Father in heaven while He was in the Garden of Gethsemane, just before His crucifixion - "I have revealed you to those whom you gave me out of the world. They were yours; you gave them to me and they have obeyed your word. Now they know that everything you have given me comes from you. For I gave them the words you gave me, and they accepted them. They knew with certainty that I came from you and they believed that that you sent me." – John 17:6-8

Jesus said that He gave us all that was given to Him. Now, we are prepared to go out into this world to make a difference and reveal the new covenant, Jesus goes on to say that He is sending us out into the world to reveal the new covenant. If you are a "Christian", Jesus defined your mission!!!

Then during the same prayer time, Jesus made a continuation of that prayer in the Garden of Gethsemane just prior to going to his death – John 17:18,19 "As you sent me into the world, I have sent them into the world. For them I sanctify myself, that they, too, may be truly sanctified." Jesus said that God sent him into this world to prepare us to go out unto the world to reveal all that God wants the world to know about Him and His standards of righteousness. Wow! That compels us to go out unto the world and do what we are called to do with our God-given gifts.

CONCLUSION: After studying the bible, after traveling all over the world to see all of God's people, after feeling His passion for the least of these, after seeing the revelation of His truth through the scriptures, after realizing the fact that the new covenant between men and God is only going to be revealed by His chosen, people, after this and more, I am convinced that one of the purest forms of worshipping Jesus is not by singing in the choir, attending church week after week, going from one bible study to another, speaking in tongues, making baptism an issue, etc., but the purest form of worship is by helping other people, by showing His love and going out unto your family, friends, country and to the world to teach His word according to the Bible and to do His works and to live the life He has called us to live. Jesus loves His people, not the things of this world. Jesus wants to show His love to the world through Christians who will demonstrate His love. You may disagree, agree, or take exception to that, but it does not matter. I believe that is what the bible teaches. And I believe it. By the way, if you want to know for sure that you belong to Him, read

I John 2:3-6: "We know that we have come to know him <u>if</u> we obey his commands. The man who says, 'I know him', but does <u>not</u> do what he commands, is a liar, and the truth is <u>not</u> in him. But if anyone obeys his Word, God's love is truly made complete in him. This is how <u>we know</u> we are in him: Whoever claims to live in him, must walk as Jesus did."

> I John 3:16-19:" This is how we know what love is: Jesus Christ laid down his life for us. And we ought to lay down our lives for our brothers. If anyone has material possessions and sees his brother in need but has no pity on him, how can the love of God be in him? Dear children, let us not love with words or tongue but with actions and in truth. This then is how we know that we belong to the truth, and how we set our hearts at rest in his presence.

These verses are from the instruction of God through His words in His bible. Do not take these verses lightly since they will direct our eternal destiny.

ACTS OF FORGIVENESS

Wrong deeds can be forgiven in one of two ways. The Bible says that Jesus is the only mediator between God and man, and that God is the only one who can forgive sins. Through His shed blood, Jesus provided the way for man to go directly to God and ask forgiveness for his sins. A human being can forgive offenses done to each other, but only God can forgive the sin of the wrongdoing.

In my discussions with believers of certain religions, I have asked how the institutionalized priest, pastor, or church leader can forgive sin. Their responses differ. Some believe the leader can actually forgive the sin. There are some that believe Mary (the mother of Jesus) can forgive sin. Others quote their leader as teaching that a priest, pastor, or church leader cannot forgive sin itself. However, by the confession of sin to the leader and the leader's committing the sin is forgiven, then the sin is forgiven. The church leader justifies this position by Paul's act of forgiveness in II Cor. 2: vs. 10, "If you forgive him, I will also forgive him." If you read the scriptures, you will see that Paul was not speaking in the text of sin against God. He was literally referring to ungodly offenses against another person. And he said, "If you people forgive him, so will I." A man had committed incest. Paul rebuked him. The man corrected his wrongs but his shame was causing him anguish and affliction. Paul was asking the Corinthians to help and love him. And he went on to say, "If you forgive him, so will I."

Teaching that any mortal man (be it priest, pastor or leader) can forgive sin can be dangerous to the souls of people. Only God can forgive sin. God forgives sin by grace through the spilt blood of Jesus Christ.

FORGIVING OTHERS: Perhaps one of the most difficult commands of Jesus is to forgive others "from the heart". To forgive "from the heart" means to forgive in the same way that God has forgiven us. Do we really understand what it really means "to forgive from the heart"? The scripture refers to an example.

Matthew 18 vs. 21-35 – "Then Peter came to Jesus and asked, "Lord, how many times shall I forgive my brother when he sins against me? Up to seven times?" Jesus answered, "I tell you, not seven times, but seventy-seven times. "Therefore, the kingdom of heaven is like a king who wanted to settle accounts with his servants. As he began the settlement, a man who owed him ten thousand talents was brought to him. Since he was not able to pay, the master ordered that he and his wife and his children and all that he had to be sold to repay the debt.

"The servant fell on his knees before him. 'Be patient with me' he begged, 'and I will pay back everything' The servant's master took pity on him, canceled the debt and let him go. "But when the servant went out, he found one of his fellow servants who owed him a hundred denarii. He grabbed him and began to choke him. 'Pay back what you owe me!' he demanded. His fellow servant fell to his knees and begged him, 'Be patient with me, and I will pay you back.' "But he refused. Instead, he went off and had the man thrown into prison until he could pay the debt. When the other servants saw what had happened, they were greatly distressed and went and told their master everything that had happened. "Then the master called the servant in. 'You wicked servant,' he said, 'I canceled all that debt of yours because you begged me to. Shouldn't you have had mercy on your fellow servant just as I had mercy on you? In his anger his master turned him over to the jailers until he should pay back all he owed."This is how my heavenly Father will treat each of you unless you <u>forgive your brother from your heart</u>."

The New Testament Greek word for "forgiveness" literally means "to let go", to "send away", or to "cancel a debt owed". Letting go is very hard when we have been offended. We naturally want to hold fast to our need to get even, to our "right" to be angry. Anger, for a season, may feel good. But, the "feel good" soon goes away and a person is left with bitterness.

Bitterness is what holds us captive and will control the joy of the day and the hope of tomorrow. If this downward spiral is left unchecked, it will lead to depression and can ultimately lead to suicide. Forgiveness from the heart is the <u>only</u> provision God has for the healing of the emotional wounds of anger and bitterness brought on by offenses of any kind.

Many times we think we have forgiven someone because they have hurt us. We think we have forgiven them; but have we really forgiven them? The thought of the offense still stirs up hurt and anger. That hurt or anger that stirred up is evidence that the forgiveness was not "from the heart". What does "from the heart" mean? Ephesians 4:32 tells us that we are to forgive <u>just as</u> "God, in Christ, has forgiven you". From studying the scriptures on how God forgives, you will find that God forgave us

> while we were still sinning
> before we admitted our sin
> before we asked for forgiveness
> completely
> unconditionally (holding back nothing from us)

Many times you will hear someone say something like "I have forgiven so and so, but I will not be around him any more". That attitude shows that the forgiveness was not "from the heart" as God requires. **Question** - How does God treat us after He has forgiven us, when we sin? It is as if the sin had never happened! Wow!! A good test to see if you really have forgiven someone who has wronged you is to examine how you treat that person. Do you withhold love or kindness from that person? Do you withdraw, either emotionally or physically? If so, then you have not forgiven "from the heart". Forgiveness "from the heart" brings about God's grace to love and to be kind to those who hurt us. Question - Is this hard to do? - Yes, but with the help of Jesus, it can be done.

Matthew 18:21-15 tells us when we do not forgive as God forgives us, He will send the tormentors. That seems harsh. But, forgiveness is the message of the Cross and God will do what He must do to bring us to forgiveness "from the heart". He does this out of His love for us. Forgiveness is for the one who has been offended.

Dr. Chuck Swindoll says this about forgiveness: "The escape route out of the prison of bitterness is clearly marked. It leads to the cross—where the only One who had a right to be bitter—wasn't." He also says this about forgiveness: "There is not torment like the inner torment of an unforgiving spirit. I am convinced that a person is far more miserable in his own bitterness than he was by the offense which caused the bitterness to develop. When you forgive, you throw wide the prison doors and then realize that the prisoner was—You!"

Why is forgiveness so hard? Consider this—for the most part people are pretty selfish and self-serving. Most of what is considered an offense that needs forgiveness is because somebody did not do something the way I wanted it done or whatever was done did not serve me the way I wanted to be served. Simply stated, most offenses become offenses because I want it my way and it did not go my way. A true servant is hardly ever offended, which requires no forgiveness. A person who wants to be served is easily offended and demands forgiveness. The next and most important reason that forgiveness is so hard is because, as mentioned earlier, forgiveness is the message of the cross. Satan knows that and will do all that he can to prevent forgiveness "from the heart". Jesus is the only one who tells us we can forgive ...but Satan hates forgiveness from the heart because Jesus, on the cross, forgave from His heart. On the cross, Jesus asked God to forgive the very ones who crucified Him. (And that included you and me, not just the Roman soldiers.) They did not ask for nor deserve that forgiveness. Because Jesus did that for us, it grieves the heart of God when we won't forgive "from our hearts". Satan can also use our pride to try to hinder us from completely forgiving. Pride can be at the root of all conditional forgiveness.

The ultimate purpose of God wanting us to forgive just as He forgives us is so that He may be glorified. When you agree to go beyond mental assent of forgiveness and bless the one who hurt you, the life of Jesus is revealed in you. And that is what brings glory to God. Colossians 3 vs. 12-13 sums it up pretty good.

Colossians 3 vs. 12-13 - Therefore, as God's chosen people, holy and dearly loved, clothe yourselves with compassion, kindness, humility, gentleness and patience. Bear with each other and forgive whatever grievances you may have against one another. Forgive as the Lord forgave you.

AMOS

The book of Amos is very interesting and can possibly give us an insight and application to our culture that we have evolved into and the results of this evolution on our destiny.

Amos – He was a sheep herder and tended to the fruit trees. God took him from his occupation and sent him to His people as a prophet. This is interesting because God works in a similar way today. God calls everybody to be a prophet of His righteousness and to be His witness. But, to some, he calls them out to reprimand apathy and laziness and then to motivate God's people to action. God is an <u>action</u> God. Jesus set the example. Jesus prepared His disciples for action to go out into the world to teach God's righteousness and to serve His people. A personal relationship with Jesus Christ and his scriptures prepares us to go into the world for the cause of God through Jesus Christ. Jesus died to fulfill that purpose.

Amos was called to go to God's people and to warn them that God did not appreciate their laziness and apathy. God blessed His people with riches and comfort and convenience and safety, but they did not use these blessings to glorify God's purpose, but to glorify their own purposes. God sent Amos to notify His people of the consequences of their misuse of His blessings.

I believe God is calling our nation to come back to Him just as he did in Amos' time. As it says in the book of Romans, chapter one, if we turn away from Him, He will turn us over to our reprobate minds and reprobate actions. The evidence of a culture that has a reprobate mind is defining itself by its actions more and more each day. These evidences are showing up in our culture and are demonstrating themselves in the social acceptance of the homosexual movement, total self indulgences and changes in our basic moral values, such as abortion and deceptions towards truth and the perception of truth. Those who cannot see this move to a reprobate mind are blinded by Satan's lies. Amos came to his people with a message from God. The same message has a huge application to the people of the United States today. Read Amos 6:1-7:

> "Woe to you who are complacent in Zion and to you who feel secure on Mount Samaria, you notable men of the foremost nation, to whom the people of Israel come! Go to Calneh and look at it; go from there to great Hamath and then go down to Gath in Philistia. Are you better than those kingdoms? Was their land larger than yours? You put off the evil day and bring near a reign of terror. You lie on beds inlaid with ivory and lounge on your couches. You dine on choice lambs and fattened calves. You strum away on your harps like David and improvise on musical instruments. You drink wine by the bowlful and use the finest lotions, but you do not grieve over the ruin of Joseph. Therefore you will be among the first to go into exile; your feasting and lounging will end".

Religiosity and Ritualism – God blessed His people beyond their needs and desires. Instead of using those assets to glorify God's name and plan, the people used those blessings to indulge themselves and to glorify themselves. Most of the people who call themselves Christians today and most of the churches who call themselves the bride of Christ are doing the same thing that God's people were doing back in the days of Amos. God used Amos to warn the people of his day. I believe God is calling on the people of this day to beware. In chapter five of Amos, God called on His people to repent and to come back to Him in <u>love and actions</u>. They did not do it, and His people were victims of God's anger. Read Amos, chapters 7-9. I believe there is a message for us because we are living in similar circumstances as the time of Amos. Note: God does not want a ritualistic relationship with man. God wants a personal and passionate relationship with man. He wants that relationship so personal and passionate that it will compel us to go out into the world and reveal what a wondrous God He is. WOW! What a wonderful God! Let us be the Christians God meant us to be. Let us go out beyond ourselves, even to all corners of the world, to proclaim the Lord, saying He is our Almighty God. Read what and how God views religiosity and ritualism. Red Amos, chapter 5:18-27 with special attention to <u>verses 21-23:</u>

> 18 "Woe to you who long for the day of the Lord! Why do you long for the day of the Lord? That day will be darkness, not light. 19 It will be as though a man fled from a lion only to meet a bear, as though he entered his house and rested his hand on the wall only to have a snake bite him. 20 Will not the day of the Lord be darkness, not light, but pitch-dark without a ray of brightness? 21 I hate, <u>I despise your religious feasts; I cannot stand your assemblies.</u> 22 <u>Even though you bring me burnt offerings and</u>

grain offerings, I will not accept them. Though you bring choice fellowship offerings, I will have no regard for them. 23 Away with the noise of your songs! I will not listen to the music of your harps. 24 But let justice roll on like a river, righteousness like a never-failing stream. 25 Did you bring me sacrifices and offerings forty years in the desert, O house of Israel? 26 You have lifted up the shrine of your king, the pedestal of your idols, the star of your god which you made for yourselves. 27 Therefore, I will send you into exile beyond Damascus, says the Lord, whose name is God Almighty."

God could see through all of the acts of religiosity and ritualism. God knew that these people were not seeking a personal relationship with Him, but rather, doing religious things to appease Him. God considers religiosity and ritualism a shallow substitute for the real things. The Lord God says woe to those who approach Him with anything other than a personal relationship. The day the Lord returns will be a dark day for those who do not seek to know Him personally. Jesus, with His sermon on the mountain, said the same thing, as recorded in Matthew 7:21-23:

21 Not everyone who says to me 'Lord, Lord' will enter the kingdom of heaven, but only he who does the will of my Father who is in heaven. 22. Many will say to me on that day, 'Lord, Lord, did we not prophesy in your name and in your name drive out demons and perform many miracles?' 23 Then I will tell them plainly, 'I never knew you. Away from me, you evil doers!'"

Give God what He is looking for, and that is a partner-servant relationship bound and certified by the blood of Jesus. Conclusion: If you see what I see, then let us get into action. The God I know, the Jesus I know, is an action God. To do nothing with your relationship with God is a huge sin.

ARE WE PART OF GOD'S BLESSING?

<u>Give to the poor</u> –
Matthew 19:21 - "Jesus told him, "If you want to be perfect, go and sell everything you have and give the money to the poor, and you will have treasure in heaven; and come, follow me.""

Galatians 2:10 - "The only thing they did suggest was that we must always remember to help the poor, and I too, was eager for that."

<u>Blessings</u> – Since blessings are a manifestation of our perception of what is good and bad, his standard of "good" is of absolute importance. Otherwise, we could be blessed and not even know it. Worse yet, we could perceive things as a blessing that are simply a function of our own works. A simple measurement that can be used to distinguish true blessings is this: Are the attributes in my life elevating me or are they elevating God? Is it all about "me" or is it all about serving others? Do I arrange circumstances to serve me, or do I arrange circumstances to serve God by serving others? We are truly blessed if we understand that God created us to find joy by serving others instead of our self. The life of Jesus was the ultimate example of that blessing in serving. He sat the standard. Remember, the old covenant was DUTY driven, whereas the new covenant is DESIRE driven. WHAT we do is important, but, more important is WHY we are doing it. I have written a paper comparing the old covenant with the new covenant that explains this in more

detail. That explanation gives more detail in the book I wrote Something to Consider.

In summary, consider carefully what you consider blessings from God. Do they draw you closer to Jesus in humility by serving others? Or, do they elevate you in your own eyes or in the eyes of others? If our works do not cause us to be more intimate with God and if our works in serving others does not elevate our God, then these works may not be blessings in God's eyes, but works of self elevation.

ASK, SEEK AND KNOCK . . . Matthew 7:7-12

"Ask and it will be given you; seek and you will find; knock and the door will be opened to you. For everyone who asks, receives; he who seeks, finds; and to him who knocks, the door will be opened. Which of you, if his son asks for bread, will give him a stone? Or, if he asks for a fish, will given him a snake? If you, then, though you are evil, know how to give good gifts to your children, how much more will your Father in heaven give good gifts to those who ask him? So, in everything, do to others what you would have them do to you, for this sums up the law and the prophets."

Commentary – Ask, Seek and Knock – These verses were given by Jesus as the way to have a relationship with Him. Jesus used the verbs ask, seek and find. Question – ask and seek what? The answer is evident in verse `12 – "So in everything, do to others what you would have them do to you, for this sums up the Law and the prophets". Ask and seek how to find His standard of righteousness and to do something. Do unto others. Make your life an action of witness of God's righteousness and of doing His good works. Once you understand what you are <u>asking</u> for and know what you are to be <u>seeking</u>, then <u>knock</u> on that door (His door) and the door will be opened. Note: There are so many who come to Jesus who are looking for a God will serve their daily <u>needs</u> and <u>desires</u> and they have no intention of giving anything back. They want a God that they can leverage to serve their own best interest. Jesus came to us as a servant to demonstrate how we <u>must</u> serve. Jesus came to prepare us to go out into the world. Question: which God are we looking for? – A God who requires us to serve (Jesus) or another type of God?

Remember, if we call ourselves Christians, then our whole basis of life should be centered around the standard of righteousness established by Jesus, as well as, the model He established as the purpose and the way of living. He came to model the way of life for a Christian. The way we live, what we believe and what we do has eternal consequences.

Remember, the standard that determines eternal judgment are not a person's standard, nor a church's standard, not a preacher's standard, but <u>only</u> God's standard set forth in His bible.

BLESSINGS AND BLESSED

Matthew 5 is often called "The Sermon on the Mount". Jesus spent a great deal of time detailing those things for which we are "blessed". The Greek word for "blessed" is makarios, which means "supremely fortunate", "well off". Consider the list below which Jesus included in blessings. It is not what most people or the world would consider being "well off" or "supremely blessed". In the eyes of Jesus, these are the properties of being blessed.

Jesus said:

"Blessed are:THE POOR IN SPIRIT – for theirs is the kingdom of heaven.

THOSE WHO MORN – for they will be comforted. THE MEEK – for they will inherit the earth. THOSE WHO HUNGER AND THIRST AFTER RIGHTEOUSNESS – for they will be filled. THE PURE IN HEART – for they will see God. THE PEACEMAKERS - for they will be called sons of Gods. THOSE WHO ARE PERSECUTED FOR RIGHTEOUS SAKE – for theirs is the kingdom of heaven."

AND THEN JESUS SAID:

"Blessed are you when people insult you and say all manner of evil against you falsely for my sake. REJOICE AND BE GLAD because great is your reward in heaven..."

Notice in every characteristic of a blessing or being blessed, the property of selflessness or self denial is required. Jesus came to provide the blood for the redemption of our sin and to demonstrate how mankind could live in total harmony. All of mankind would live in harmony if all of mankind would possess these properties of blessed or blessings as expressed by Jesus.

BLESSINGS AND MIRACLES

What an interesting subject! What is a blessing and/or miracle? Each term can be basically simple, but each can be made complex depending on the intent and application of the word. There are three methods to evaluate the intent and function of a word, or series of words: the theoretical, the philosophical and the theological. Listed below is a description of each:

Theoretical – a hypothesis (explanation) drawn from speculation. For this reason, theory is not used to study biblical terms and meanings.

Philosophical – a hypothesis drawn from what is believed to be truth or fact. There has to be a reason to believe some form of fact was used to derive the hypothesis. Philosophy can be used to study bible terms, but is most often not used. The reason why philosophy is not normally used is because most of the concepts used in the bible deal, to a large degree, with the element of faith. A large part of the Christian belief system is based on faith. If you are not a Christian, how can you explain the non-tangible power and force of the Holy Spirit? Faith is a key element in the Christian persuasion, and that, in itself, excludes it from the definition of philosophical.

Theological – a hypothesis drawn from what is believed to be true from factal and non-factual evidence to derive a conclusion. The Christian faith derives conclusion from hard, irrefutable evidence and from evidences that are believed to be fact.

For the sake of this study, we will use the theological approach.

Blessings. Blessings, as defined in the Old Testament using the Hebrew word **brakah**, means "a benediction", or as defined in street talk language – a divine favor given by God on a person of His choice. This divine favor can come as a reward for obedience, or the divine favor can come in the form of praise or approval. The most obvious application of this definition comes in Deuteronomy 11: 26-28.

Deuteronomy 11:26-28 – "See, I am setting before you a blessing and a curse – the blessing if you obey the commands of the Lord your God that I am giving you today – the curse if you disobey the commands of the Lord your God and turn from the way that I command you today by following other gods which you have not know.

At this point, I want to draw an obvious conclusion when you use the Hebrew definition. Blessings come only from a divine origin. If you, by your own time and energy, cause or alter an event, most likely it is a function of your own ambition. God can bless you with the ability to do something to cause a desired event, but if you are not doing the event for God's sake or not following God's lead, it is probable the event is a function of your own ambition. Remember, God <u>desires</u> things to happen, and He also <u>allows</u> things. He may allow it, but He also may not desire it. Example, it is hard to say that God blessed me with a car, <u>if</u> the car was a function of my own self-serving desire. God did not bless me with the car; He allowed me to have it. It was my ambition to have the car, not His.

Some of God's blessings can be immediately understood, and some blessings will be understood at a later time, and some blessings may slip by us without us recognizing the blessings, and other blessings cannot be understood immediately. God is in charge of all blessings – not man.

Miracles. Miracles are blessings that are immediate and easily understood as a divine intervention of God. They have a desired outcome. Example: God ordains that a blind man can see, or a cripple can walk. Those blessings are immediate and easy to understand because they have a desired outcome. Do I believe in miracles? Yes, yes, yes! God can choose to do what He desires. And it may not be what we approve of or understand. God does what He does for His own reasons. **What?** God does what He does for His own reasons? Yep! A clear testament to that fact is found in Romans 9. I challenge you to read the whole chapter.

> **Romans 9:14-16** – "What then shall we say? Is God unjust? Not at all! For he says to Moses, 'I will have mercy on whom I have mercy, and I will have compassion on whom I have compassion.'

It does not, therefore, depend on man's desire or effort, but on God's mercy."

Going back to the subject of blessings, outlined below are some questions I have been challenged with regarding blessings, along with what I have derived from my study of the scriptures on the subject:

What does God consider the most important blessing to us as His people? The greatest blessing is that He dwells within us. Also, in Romans 10:15, Hebrews 9:11 and Hebrews 10:1, the goodness of God's blessing refers to the benefits provided through the sacrifice of Christ, in regard both to these things conferred through the gospel for all believers now and to those things which will come with the Messianic Kingdom. Psalm 3:8 says that God's blessing is upon His people through salvation.

What is known as the first blessing? The first occurrence of this blessing is when God blessed Abraham. God's blessings rest on those who are faithful to Him. His blessings bring

righteousness – Psalm 24:5
life – Psalm 133:3
salvation – Psalm 3:8
prosperity – God can bless with possessions – II Samuel 7:29

Does God bless us at times and we don't recognize it or know it? Yes, more often than we realize it, God is blessing us or has blessed us and we missed it. How can that be? Remember, the blessing of a miracle is usually predictable and immediately desired. Other blessings may come in a form that is unexpected. Too often we put conditions on God and try to transact with God – **If you love me, you will perform in the form of my expected behavior. Another is – Before I will consider it blessing, the outcome should occur in the way I want it.**

Let me give an example of the greatest blessing of God to mankind that was messed up by His people. God promised

His first chosen, the Jews, a Messiah who would have been the greatly prophesized blessing. The blessing was that the Messiah was to be a conquering warrior. The Jews misjudged and predetermined the form of the Messiah, and the form that was to be used to conquer. God sent Jesus, not a warrior of war who would shed the blood of others, but as a warrior of sacrifice, who would give His blood for others. As it says in Hebrews, conquering by war did not work. Jesus came to set a new standard and a new method. His people will conquer by love through giving and forgiving. The first chosen, the Jews, missed the blessing because they had

Predetermined what they would receive as a blessing. Because of that, they have never had the gifts- joy or peace. That should be a clear lesson for us all to learn. God is blessing us every day. Our joy, peace and sense of self worth is directly correlated to our belief in that. Remember, the greatest blessing that we as Christians have ever received is when God came to live within each of us through the person of the Holy Spirit. If that was the only blessing we would ever receive, it would be enough!

What are our expectations and perceptions of blessings? The Lord has allowed me to visit many other countries on mission trips. When I return, I am amazed to see how God has set this land in the USA apart from the rest of the world and allowed it to be blessed. I know in my heart of hearts that this land was blessed because it was founded on Christian principles. The name and Word of God was woven into every legal document. God's name even appears on our currency. That same blessing has not shown up in any other country. What we take for granted here in the USA would be considered a blessing anywhere outside the borders of the USA. What is considered a poverty and waste here in the USA is considered a blessing in most other countries. I have been in many church services in Central and South America where the people were thanking God for things like a glass of clean water, a half-spoiled apple, or a piece of tin metal they could use as shelter and considering them blessings. Many of these people are diseased, tired and hungry, but yet they find joy, peace, contentment and a sense of self-worth because they give thanks for all things and consider all things a gift or blessing from God. Because of what I have seen, my life has changed, and I try to be thankful for even the smallest things that life has to offer. I have the ability to make a choice. I will choose to consider all things as a blessing from God. I choose to be grateful for what God allows me to have, rather than to murmur over what I do not have. The most special blessing is the Holy Spirit who lives in me.

Conclusion - It has been fun and enlightening to study what God considers as a blessing. I have found that many individuals have used the term and concept of blessing as a tool to justify their own greed and self-gratification. Their hypothesis, or thought process, goes like this – God must love me because the more He loves me, the more He gives me for my own self-indulgence. That may have been true under the first covenant, but it is not o true under the New Covenant. Under the New Covenant, all blessings are given to glorify His name, not our name. We are to use those gifts and blessings to show His love to others through giving and forgiving. We, as Christians, should find joy, peace and sense of divine purpose because He is in control. Therefore, there are three things that should be derived from all blessings and miracles. God does blessings and miracles in our lives for three reasons. The three reasons are

 *** Righteousness – knowing what God values as right and wrong and knowing God's will for our life to serve His purpose.

 *** Holiness – doing God's will for good and His purpose.

*** Intimacy – God wants to have an intimate love relationship with His people.

BOASTING IN WEAKNESS

Some years ago, I listened to a tape from Dr. Moses Caesar. Dr. Moses Caesar came to Auburn Baptist Church to give a COMMUNICATION OF TRUTH message about who Jesus really is and what the life of a Christian <u>must</u> be. It was a very revealing message about how God views the life of a Christian. After that message, I gleaned some thoughts I would like to share.

There are a lot of preachers who are professional orators; who are preaching religion for the purpose of selling religion for the sake of self gain and the collection plate. (These are my thoughts, not Dr. Caesar's) One of the methods used to sell religion is through the theory that God is obligated to serve each person by fulfilling his desires. In essence, you were put here on earth so that God could serve you. The driving force of this thought process goes like this: Whatever your desires are, if you have enough faith, God will fulfill your desires because He is obligated to do so. Basically, they are saying that God is an instrument in their hands and if they have enough faith and if they believe in their own desires, God must do what they are ordering Him to do through a belief system and a faith system. What a delusion and illusion of the real truth. Read II Corinthians 11 and 12. Starting in chapter 11 with verse 16, Paul goes through the scenario of his life. He records all the times he was beaten to near death. He was stoned and he was whipped with a cat of nine tails forty-nine times. He was shipwrecked three times. His life story is one of a lot of cruel punishment. His punishment was for taking his stand to believe and defend Jesus Christ. Everything that Jesus preached about was to <u>serve others</u> and to be <u>selfless</u>. The world wants to be served. It does not want to serve. Therefore, they reject the true message of Jesus. Jesus set the standard and the example

41

for our walk with Him. His example was to <u>give and forgive</u> as pointed out several times in the book <u>Something to Consider</u>. Paul came to know the real persona and the real passion of Jesus and that was to serve by giving and forgiving. Paul went on to deliver that passionate message of and about Jesus even though it was at the expense of his own body. Later in Chapter 12, starting with verse7:

Later in Chapter 12, starting with verse 7:

"To keep me from becoming conceited because of these surpassingly great revelations, there was given to me a thorn in my flesh, a messenger of Satan, to torment me. (8) Three times I pleaded with the Lord to take it away from me. (9) But He said to me, 'My grace is sufficient for you, for my power is made perfect in weakness.' Therefore, I will boast all the more gladly about my weaknesses, so that Christ's power may rest on me. (10) That is why, for Christ's sake, I delight in weaknesses, in insults, in hardships, in persecutions in difficulties. For when I am weak, then I am strong.'"

Take note: Paul said, "I am only strong in my weaknesses." That is not the message the world has to offer. The world teaches strength in power. This power can be an instrument for control. This control then can be used to serve self rather than to serve others.

Notice in these verses, Paul was referring to boasting. In the verses prior to these verses, Paul was going through a dissertation on "what is worth boasting about and what is not worth boasting about." He is pointing out the difference between a self-serving boasting and a God-serving boasting. He culminates this subject of boasting. Look at the verses starting with verse 7 in Chapter 12. Notice after reading these verses, Paul talks of three times he pleaded with the Lord to take away from him the thorn in his flesh. But Paul came to realize the thorn was actually put there by God, Himself, to keep him humbled. After Paul realized that God placed the thorn in his flesh, this thorn in his flesh was really a blessing. He rejoiced in the thorn and he boasted in the thorn. He realized that the thorn kept him weak and God can only use people in their weakness rather than in their strength. Paul rejoiced with the thorn. He rejoiced because he knew that if he understood the purpose of the thorn and with that purpose comes the afflictions of the thorn and the agony, pain, and adversity that comes with the thorn, then this thorn would have great value in the eyes of the Lord. Paul knew that life is not perfect. Paul knew what this world has to offer can be cruel and full of hardships and pain. But, if you use those thorns to glorify the Lord, the thorns will have value in God's eternal plan.

There seems to be so many people over obsessed about whether they feel good or feel bad. Unfortunately, that is true of most Christians. Their perspective is short term. Their life efforts are committed to self. They use all this world has to offer to gratify self. Many of them are deceived in believing that God blesses people for their own vain comforts. They want to believe that the more faith they have the more God blesses them. There is absolutely nothing further from the truth than that. God does not give things to us to glorify our flesh. If He gives us anything at all, it is to make us a living example of His Grace. It is my observation that most people with a lot of possessions and wealth become self absorbed and self proclaimed prophets of their worthiness before God.

Analyze what Paul has said in these verses, "let us not boast in our strength, but boast only in our weakness." God does not use man in his strength, lest he boast about his strength. God only uses man in his weakness.

There is a great lesson to be learned from the example of Paul's life and from what Paul has observed about his Christian walk. It is interesting to note that Paul wrote this letter to the Corinthians in the latter part of his ministry when he had an opportunity to experience all that could happen to him and he had gone through a high level of maturity and fully understood the heart and the passion of the Lord Jesus Christ. This letter is a passion letter from God to His people, using Paul as the example.'

Dr. Moses Caesar pointed out that Paul had discovered the secret of the Lord's perspective of all things. The Lord's perspective is from an eternal point of view and we too often look at everything from a temporary point of view. Our sufferings are only temporary and if we serve the Lord through those sufferings, then the pain is only a temporary pain. Our mission here on earth is to endure the small pains, the small disappointments in life from the perspective that all these go together to serve an eternal purpose. We should be glad and honored to be part of God's eternal purpose, especially if it involves pain and suffering. The bigger question is <u>NOT</u> "why do I have these thorns?", but the big question is "why have You (God) trusted me with these thorns to glorify you?"

COMMANDMENTS GIVEN BY GOD

The commandments given by God are amazing. The commandments are commands that offer no other choice or alternative. They are to be obeyed. Notice the prevailing intent behind each command. The intent behind each command is to offer a way for man to live in total harmony with each other. Every command is centered around loving your family and neighbors. Actually, each command is a sacrifice of the sinful nature to serve self. Each command is also an order of respect and reverence to God and fellowman. Some will say these commands are God's laws and maybe they are. But, actually, they are a definition of the character of God. These commands define the character and person of God. They also define God's desire toward the creation of his people. Study these commands and see what you think.

The Old Covenant Commandments

The Ten Commandments given by God to Moses for the people of the First Covenant Dispensation – Exodus 20:3-17:

1. "You shall have no other God's before me."
2. "You shall not make for yourself an idol in the form of anything in heaven above or on the earth beneath or in the waters below. You shall not bow down to them or worship them, for I, the Lord your God, am a jealous God, punishing the children for the sin of the fathers to the third and fourth generation of those who hate me, but showing love to the thousands who love me and keep my commandments."
3. "You shall not misuse the name of the Lord your God, for the Lord will not hold anyone guiltless who misuses His name."
4. "Remember the Sabbath day by keeping it holy. Six days you shall labor and do all your work, but the seventh day is a Sabbath to the Lord your God. On it you shall not do any work, neither you, nor your son or daughter, nor your manservant or maidservant, nor your animals, nor the alien within your gates. For in six days the Lord made the heavens and the earth, the seas and all that is in them, but He rested on the seventh day. Therefore the Lord blessed the Sabbath and made it holy."
5. "Honor your father and your mother, so that you may live long in the land the Lord your God is giving you."
6. "You shall not murder."
7. "You shall not commit adultery."
8. "You shall not steal."
9. "You shall not give false testimony against your neighbor."
10. "You shall not covet your neighbor's house. You shall not covet your neighbor's wife, or his manservant or

maidservant, his ox or donkey, or anything that belongs to your neighbor."

The New Covenant Commandments

The three commandments given by God for Jesus for the people of the New Covenant Dispensation:
First two commandments – Matthew 22:36-40:
"Teacher, what is the greatest commandment in the Law? Jesus replied,

1. "Love the Lord your God with all your heart and with all your soul and with all your mind. This is the first and greatest commandment.

2. And the second is: 'Love your neighbor as yourself.' All the Law and the Prophets hang on these two commandments."

The third commandment given by Jesus – John 13:34-35:

3. "A new commandment I give you. 'Love one another' as I have loved you, so you must love one another. All men will know that you are my disciples if you love one another.

Think about the depth of these commandments. They require that we love God *above* all things and by self denial to love others by freely giving and forgiving because God loves us so much that He gave His only Son to die on the cross to provide the blood that covers our sin so that we are presented perfect before God. WOW! What an expression of love! If we would do this, man could live in perfect harmony with God, himself and all other men.

Note: The words "man" and "men" includes women and children.

CRUCIFYING JESUS AGAIN AND DISGRACING HIM

Hebrews 6:4-6 - "It is impossible for those who have once been enlightened, who have tasted the heavenly gift, who have shared in the Holy Spirit, who have tasted the goodness of the word of God and the powers of the coming age, if they fall away, to be brought back to repentance, because to their loss, they are crucifying the Son of God all over again and subjecting Him to public disgrace".

The Scripture says once you have been enlightened and shared in the presence of our God and have fallen away, it is impossible to be brought back into repentance. Why? Because to their loss, they are crucifying the Son of God all over again and subjecting Him to public disgrace.

The Scripture says once you have <u>tasted</u> the <u>heavenly gift</u>, have shared in the <u>Holy Spirit</u>, have <u>tasted</u> the <u>goodness</u> of the <u>word of God</u> and the <u>powers of the coming age</u> – if you have done that, you have experienced the very presence of God in your life. When you have experienced that intimate blessing, God holds you deeply accountable. If you fall away from God after this intimate experience, repentance is impossible. This teaching makes it very clear that God requires a commitment to Him.

FIRST JOHN 3:9

I John 3:9

"No one who is born of God will continue to sin because God's seed remains in him; he cannot go on sinning because he has been born of God".

47

To understand this verse and its context, it would be good to know about John. John was a man who enjoyed a totally committed fellowship with God. His life and commitment to God was 100%. His concept of a relationship with God was 100% for himself and anybody else who walked with God. John saw God as the God of light, love and the God of life. His concern for the followers of Jesus was related to false teachers. The false teachers were those people that were greatly influenced by the world and all of its ways to pull the followers from their relationship and commitment to God. His opinion was so intense that he felt there was no deviation from a total, 100% commitment to God. There was no room for sin if you love God.

Then, in chapter 4, Paul says we are sinners! Why does this exist? I do not know. There are some things that God wants to be kept a mystery. There is a scripture in the Old Testament which says, "The secret things belong to God. What he wants us to know, he will show us". <u>There is one thing I do know. It is not good to dwell on those things we do not understand, but to dwell on those things that we do understand.</u> There is one passage that reveals God in His entirety –

John 3:16: "For God so loved the world that he gave his only son that whosoever believes in him will not perish but have everlasting life".

If we focus on that verse every day, and let it sink into our heart and soul, those verses that are not easily understood will not matter.

By the way, the Bible commentators feel like that series in I John was referring to your sinful life prior to being saved and also sins that we do not repent of, instead of any form of sin.

Now, you mentioned that you have never known a time that Jesus came into your life and you made Him Lord of your life – a specific time. You have always known of Him and even feel His presence in your heart. Jesus said we must be born again. That means to me that there is a specific time that a person commits to Him. It is my feeling that if a person has always had an awareness of God, but never made a specific commitment to His Son Jesus, then maybe that born again experience has never happened. Born again means the death of the old person and the birth of a new person that is committed to God through His son Jesus.

FROM CREATION TO SALVATION

Why has God chosen to reveal to me the story of "Creation to Salvation" for me to present the plan of salvation? Others do a great job using other methods to explain the plan of salvation. As for me, however, the story of "Creation to Salvation" demonstrates the reason for the origin of sin, the reason for the penalty of sin and the only solution for the forgiveness of sin so that we are made acceptable before God. God has allowed me to go over a large part of the world to present this story, or a story similar to this, depending on the situation. I truly appreciate this revelation from God. Through this presentation, thousands and thousands have prayed a commitment to Jesus, the Christ. Hopefully, this will give you "something to consider".

The presentation of this story is usually not the same, but the principles are always the same. By the way, I do not quote a lot of scripture, because they cannot understand the impact of the scriptures until they accept Jesus and He reveals His truth to them. The story goes something like this:

Hello. My name is David Leatherman, and I came a long way from Tupelo, Ms to share God's love for you. He loves you that much that He would send somebody all this way to reveal a very important message so that you could find an everlasting friend and find the way to escape eternal hell and to find eternal paradise. (I hold up the Bible.)

God sent His Son to earth to demonstrate how God wants us to live together in peace and joy. He sent His Son to be the only way into heaven. Later, He sent all of this information down to us in this book, called the Bible. God has sent me to reveal His story from His book, the Bible.

In the beginning, there was nothing. God became lonely, so He created the earth. There was nothing on the earth, so He decided to make it beautiful. He is such a powerful God that He spoke everything into existence. He was so powerful that He said, "Let there be water upon the earth", and all the waters appeared. He went on to say, "Let there be all the plants of the earth", and all the plants of the earth appeared. Then he said, "Let there be all kinds of birds and animals and sea creatures", and they all appeared. He did this for all parts of the world. WOW! What a powerful God!

All of the earth was created, and He loved it, but He was still lonely, so He decided to create a "best friend". You like friends, don't you? He wanted a friend, so He reached down and grabbed a hand full of dust/dirt and He carefully formed that dirt (I demonstrate what He did) perfectly, because it was going to be His best friend. When He was satisfied, He breathed life into that dirt and the dirt became flesh that had a purpose and a soul. WOW! He was happy! What was the name of God's friend? Yes – Adam. God and Adam had a great time together in this place called the Garden of Eden. Later, Adam wanted a friend, so God created a woman for him. What was the woman's name? That is right – Eve. God, Adam and Eve were so happy. There was no work, the greatest food, not too hot and not too cold. It was perfect. God said, "You can have all of this forever, but there is a fruit that you cannot eat. If you do, you will know good and bad. Guess what happened? (I ask them what happened.) Yes, they ate the fruit. That made God very angry. They were now dirty with sin, so God threw them out of the Garden. And he turned Satan loose. Do you know who Satan is? He is the ruler of a place called hell. It is a bad place of fire and torture.

So, once again, God separated Himself from Adam and Eve and all of their descendents. Adam and Eve wanted to come back, but God said, NO; you have sinned and you are dirty and all of your descendents will be dirty with sin. By the way, you and I are descendents of Adam and Eve. We are born with a dirty heart and we are unacceptable to God because of our sinful nature given to us by Adam and Eve.

God then said there is a way to be justified with me, and it is through blood. You must cast your sins on an altar and kill a perfect animal. Use the blood of that animal to cover your sins. So, they did that. They would sin and kill an animal to use the blood. Time and again, they would sin and then kill an animal to use the blood. Time and again they would sin and then kill an animal. The problem was that they did not repent, so they committed the same sins and kept killing perfectly innocent animals.

God looked down and said, "This is not what I intended, and it is not good." So He decided to send His Son. God knew that the people would hate Him because of their sin, and they would kill Him. So, God sent His Son to earth knowing that. What was His Son's name? Yes – His name was Jesus. Jesus came to pay the blood price for our sin. Remember, God had said, "No one can come to Me except for the price of blood". Just as God had said, man killed Jesus. Do you know how man killed Jesus? (At this point, I try to demonstrate). They tied His hands to a post. Then they tied bones and stones into a whip. Then they whipped Him. When they did, the bones and stones would dig into His flesh. When they pulled the whip back, it would tear the flesh from His body. Then they beat Him with rods.

Do you know that Jesus did not have to do this? This was God's son, with all of the power that God has. He said He could have called legions of angels to rescue Him, but He did not do that. Do you know why? Because He loves you; because He loves you; because He loves you. (I point my finger at each person). He knew you would go to hell if He did not do this. Do you understand He chose to do this because He loves you? WOW! Then they took Him to the cross and laid Him on the cross. (I demonstrate how they nailed His hands and feet). They laid Him and straightened out His hand and drove a nail through his hand. (I scream like His pain must have been). Then they nailed His other hand to the cross. (I scream again). Then they nailed His feet (I scream again).

Remember – Jesus could have stopped all of this, but He didn't because He loves you; He loves you; He loves you. He hung on the cross for a long time, suffering for you. Even with all that Jesus did to this point, it was not enough. WHERE WAS THE BLOOD that God requires? So, they picked up a spear (I demonstrate this) and shoved it into His side and out came the blood. It came to the ground and the waters of the earth, and it made all things perfect. Then, Jesus died. God looked down on His Son who died on the cross and gave His blood and said, "NOW I AM SATISFIED. THIS WILL BE THE WAY FOR MAN TO COME TO ME."

So, here we are today, guilty of sin, and we are committed to go to hell unless we accept Jesus as our Savior. It is decision time – it is heaven or hell. Do you want to make a decision to follow Jesus? Before you answer that question, the Bible tells us your must decide to do three things:

1. Admit that you are a sinner. Sin can be explained simply. There are two parts. Part 1- (I demonstrate lightly hitting someone.) I cannot hurt someone. That person belongs to God. If I hurt him, I am hurting God. I cannot steal from him or talk bad about him, because he belongs to God, and that would hurt him and would also hurt God.

Part 2 – Our God is a jealous God. He said to put no other god before Him. Some people will tell you that you can worship a carved piece of wood, or a statue, or a rock. NO! God says that is sin.

2. You must believe that Jesus died on the cross and gave His blood for you. Some people will tell you that I can get you into heaven. If I could, I would have to show you the blood. Some people say that a preacher or a priest can get you into heaven. NO they cannot! They would have to show you the blood. Some people say the church or baptism can get you into heaven. NO; they would have to show you the blood. Only Jesus can get you into heaven because He gave the blood. The second thing for a way into heaven – Believe that Jesus died and gave His blood for you.

3. The third thing – Commit your life to Jesus. He wants to know you and He wants you to know Him. He created you for a great purpose and He wants you to commit yourself to Him so you can fulfill that purpose.

So, once again: One – you must confess that you are a sinner. Two – you must believe that Jesus died and gave His blood to provide forgiveness of your sins. Three – He wants you to commit to Him.

It is decision time. Are you willing and committed to do these three things? (I ask each person.) Now, if God is talking to your spirit, he asks you to go in prayer to Him and pray these three things to Him. This prayer is between God and you. You are praying to God, not me.

If you mean this in your heart, pray this prayer out loud after me. "Dear Jesus, I admit that I am a sinner, and I am sorry for my sin. Dear Jesus, I believe you died on the cross and gave your blood for my sins. Dear Jesus, I want to commit my life to You.

Dear Jesus, You said that if I prayed this prayer and meant it in my heart, that you would accept me into heaven .Dear Jesus, thank you. Amen"

Then I explain that they must pray to Him, read the Bible and go to a God-loving church.

Note: This presentation does not answer all of the questions and does not explain the resurrection. That will come.

What it does do is get them acquainted with the story of "From Creation to Salvation" and the amount of love God has for them by giving His only Son to die for them.

GOD SAID THAT VENGEANCE BELONGS TO HIM

Daily I talk to people who are perplexed by the ever growing amount of ungodliness and perversion going on in the U.S.A. They see the government indorsing and also initiating laws that destroy lives and the moral character of people. They see people choosing evil over good. Paul must have foreseen what would happen in these times. In the book of Romans, Chapter 1, he said when the government and the people turn away from God, the people will no longer be able to distinguish good from evil. Then men will be attracted to men and women will be attracted to women. Then God will turn these people over to a reprobate mind where there is no limit to sin and the destruction they will do. That is where we are today. Sin and irrational behavior abound, and these ungodly people do ungodly acts and deeds, guided by an ungodly ruler. The president of the USA declared that we are not a Christian nation, and a large portion of the people declares there is no god and walk the path of the ungodly. The government leaders give no recompense for ungodliness but actually support it. Question: Is there no punishment for this insanity? Be patient. God will avenge these grievances against his standard of righteousness. Read Romans 12:9 below:

> "Dear friends, never avenge yourselves. Leave that to God, for he has said that he will repay those who deserve it. Don't take the law into your own hands."

It is very interesting that the very first chapter of Psalms addresses this very issue. Men can fool each other, but not God.

Psalm 1 - "Oh the joys of those who do not follow evil men's advice, who do not hang around with sinners, scoffing at the things of God. But they delight in doing everything God wants them to and day and night are always meditating on his laws and thinking about ways to follow him more closely. They are like trees along a river bank bearing luscious fruit each season without fail. Their leaves shall never wither, and all they do shall prosper. But for sinners, what a different story! They blow away like chaff before the wind. They are not safe on Judgment Day; they shall not stand among the godly. For the Lord watches over all the plans and paths of godly men, but the paths of the godless lead to doom."

GOD, YOUR PERFECT PLAN IS SO PERFECT

The shortest chapter in the Bible is Psalm 117.
The longest chapter in the Bible is Psalm 119.
The chapter in the center of the Bible is Psalm 118.
There are 594 chapters before Psalm 118.
There are 594 chapters after Psalm 118.

```
   594
 + 594
Total 1,188
```

What verse is in the center of the Bible? Psalm 118:8

Psalm 118:8 – "It is better to trust in the Lord than to put your confidence in man".

Isn't it amazing that God's perfect will for the center of our life is in the center of His instruction book, the bible? If you want to find God's perfect will for your life and also how to be in the center of His will, read Psalm 118:8.God wants to be the center of your life, so He put one of His most profound statements in the center of His last known truth given to man. Psalm 118:8 – "It is better to trust in the Lord than to put your trust in man".

Satan, on the other hand, has a miserable plan for your life – a plan of "SIN", which leads to pain, disappointment, destruction, and eternal hell. His plan is all about sin. And what is in the middle of the word "SIN"? You've got it! It is "I". When Satan can get you to thinking about "I", he has got you right where he wants you. The "I" in us wants to be served and wants everything to be about "I". Jesus came to teach us to give and forgive and to serve and direct us away from "I".

THE REALITY OF ETERNITY is that the flesh lives and dies, but the spirit within you never dies. It will spend eternity in heaven or hell. Are you ready for your judgment? Heaven is forever and hell is forever.

A prayer: Dear Heavenly Father, please reveal yourself to the person reading this script, so that they will see your perfect plan and feel your perfect presence. You created a plan for each of us so that we can live a life that is created for us. You are the only source of true joy and hope here on earth and the only way to heaven. Also, reveal the consequences of hell, so that they will have a vision of eternal hell. Lord, I pray for a special blessing on their life. Amen

HABAKKUK
God Is My Refuge

Our political structure and the majority of the people have turned away from their creator, God. This nation, U.S.A., does not acknowledge its sin and therefore does not repent of its sin. Surely, God has lifted His hand off of this nation and now it belongs to the great deceiver and destroyer. Just about everybody can see and feel the hand of destruction upon them. It is coming.

Habakkuk lived in a time when Judah turned from God. Judah would not repent and turn back to God. God informed Habakkuk that He would allow the Babylonians to punish Judah for its sinful ways. Habakkuk realizes that he would be a victim of the punishment of the sin of Judah. Knowing that his life would soon be full of torment, he praises the Lord. Read Habakkuk 3:17-19:

"Though the fig tree does not bud, and there are no grapes on the vines, though the olive crop fails and the fields produce no food, though there are no sheep in the pen and no cattle in the stalls, yet I will rejoice in the Lord; I will be joyful in God, my Savior. The Sovereign Lord is my strength; he makes my feet like the feet of a deer; he enables me to go on the heights."

Note: We can generalize Habakkuk's situation to our own application of life. Here it is – We may currently be in a terrible or tormenting situation and be desperate because the problems seem to be bigger than any solution. If you are not there now, you may be there soon. What is the answer? Do what Habakkuk did. Trust in the Lord, knowing that He is sovereign and can be trusted. Habakkuk did not understand the ways of the Lord; he just trusted Him. Because of that truth, Habakkuk celebrated by praising the Lord in spite of the terrible situation. After the celebration, the situation did not seem too terrible.

Habakkuk has a lesson to teach us. Question: Is God talking to you through the lesson of Habakkuk?

HELL AND PAIN

When I was having pain due to shoulder surgery, I asked God to show me a purpose in having this pain. Because I asked, God allowed me to realize that while my pain was confined to my right shoulder, Jesus submitted to the PRICE OF PAIN all over His whole body and to the pain of sin that was cast on His spirit to cover the sin debt for all of His creation. No other man will ever know that pain. Thank you Jesus, for taking that pain away from us to cover our sin debt.

Pain – It occurred to me that as painful as this pain had been to my flesh, it would someday go away. At the very worst, the pain of my flesh will go away at my death. Question – What if this pain would never go away? What if the pain of my flesh was ten times worse than what I experienced and lasted throughout eternity? What if the pain never went away? Can that happen? Will that happen? Will pain last for eternity? Answer: the Scriptures tell us we are born of the flesh and the spirit. When we die, the pain of the flesh will go away. The spirit, however, never dies. The spirit will exist for eternity. The spirit will exist in hell (the house of pain) or in heaven (the house of rejoicing). Can you imagine the pain associated with an eternity in hell – the house of pain? Jesus suffered the PAIN DEBT so that we could live in The House of Rejoicing – HEAVEN! Each one of us is responsible for the choices in our life that will lead to our eternal destination. By the way, if we are thinking, "I just won't make a choice" - if we are thinking that way, we have actually made a choice that leads to eternal damnation. We must choose to follow Jesus.

HOSEA – GOD DEMONSTRATES HIS LOVE AND FORGIVENESS

God uses a willing servant to illustrate to Israel, and now to us, the people of this age and time, how much He loves and forgives His people. God asked Hosea to marry a known prostitute for a purpose, so he did. They had two sons. Their marriage was terrible by anybody's standard. He was faithful, like God is, and she was unfaithful by selling herself back into sin, like Israel was. Hosea had every legal and moral reason to abandon her, but he continued to love her and forgive her, just like God had every legal and moral reason to abandon Israel but chose to love and forgive Israel. God is showing this mercy and love for us as He did Israel, but for how long?

One of Israel's many sins was to substitute ritualism and ceremony for a personal relationship with God. A personal relationship results in living by God's standard of righteousness. That is exactly what is going on in the religious community, today in most cases. Hosea's life was an example of God's mercy and grace, but the Israelites were so self absorbed that they did not listen to the prophet Hosea or observe the lessons of his life. In spite of their sin, God showed mercy on Israel. I pray God that You would show the same mercy on our country (the U.S.A.) for its rebellious sins as you showed to Israel. Israel was guilty and we the people of the U.S.A. are guilty. Please show mercy and grace and help us to repent and return back to you.

Read Hosea 14:1-9 –

"Return, O Israel, to the Lord your God. Your sins have been your downfall. Take words with you and return to the Lord. Say to Him: 'Forgive all our sins and receive us graciously, that we may offer the fruit of our lips. Assyria cannot save us; we will not mount war-horses. We will never again say 'Our gods' to what our own hands have made, for in you, the fatherless find compassion.

> "I will heal their waywardness and love them freely, for my anger has turned away from them. I will be like the dew to Israel; he will blossom like a lily. Like a cedar of Lebanon, he will send down his roots; his young shoots will grow. His splendor will be like an olive tree; his fragrance like a cedar of Lebanon. Men will dwell again in his shade. He will flourish like the grain. He will blossom like a vine, and his frame will be like the wine from Lebanon.

"O Ephraim, what more have I to do with idols? I will answer him and care for him. I am like a green pine tree; your fruitfulness comes from me. Who is wise? He will realize these things. Who is discerning? He will understand them. The ways of the Lord are right; the righteous walk in them, but the rebellious stumble in them."

JOHN 14:14
"You may ask for anything in my name, and I will do it."
Quoted from the NIV Bible

This scripture is used out of context so often and it is very frightening. If you use this scripture and leave it stand on its own, by itself, then that would be a license to get anything you want. However, that's not the intent of what Jesus said. Throughout the scripture, we are told that we are called according to a purpose and to His purpose. There is a presumption, even within the Christian community, that God created us so that He could serve us, rather than the reality that God created us so that we can worship and serve Him. The context of the John 14:14 passage is this: Jesus is preparing His disciples for the fact that He will no longer be there with them. He is in the midst of revealing that He and the Holy Father are one. And he is preparing them for their mission as disciples. These disciples will go out into the mission field and serve according to their purposes. In the process of preparing His disciples, the Lord said, "Ask me for anything in my name and I will do it". The phrase "in my name" means that which is according to Christ's character and God's will. What Jesus is referring to is anything according to the disciples' mission, not for their personal gain. Do you see this is not a reference to self, but rather a means to His mission? Immediately after He tells the disciples this, He prepares them for the Holy Spirit.

Jesus further expands upon this very same subject in chapter 15. Verse 7 says "If you remain in me and my words remain in you, ask whatever you wish and it will be unto you". Again, the whole context of asking and receiving is about our mission as disciples for the Lord. Read Chapter 15:1-17. You will find that it clearly delineates that truth.

Once again, if John 14:14 is taken out of context, the presumption is that God created us so that He could serve us, which is not true at all, because God created us so that we could love and serve Him and Jesus became the example for us.

There is a fine line between our own ambition and God's desires for us. Often times, preachers, as well as lay persons, will fractionalize the scripture and will use selective passages to justify their preconceived ambitions and desires, instead of using scripture in the context of His text. God may allow man's ambition to succeed, but it doesn't mean that He desires it. In every instance in the New Testament, every reference to our asking for, and receiving, is in reference to a preparation for righteousness and holiness so that we might serve our Father as an ambassador for Him. The whole basis of blessing, changed from the Old Covenant to the New Covenant. In the Old Covenant, most, if not all, blessings were transactional. If man did something, God would bless him. In the New Covenant, we serve out of a desire, not as a duty. An example would be from the Old Testament command to honor your father and mother so that you will be blessed. The New Covenant sets forth the command to honor your father and mother because you love God and because you have already been blessed.

MATTHEW 7:7 "Ask and you will be given what you ask for".

If this verse could stand on its own, then there would be no end to what we would ask for to serve or own vanity, ambitions and desires. This verse is not intended to stand on its own. Check its context. Jesus is referring to holiness, sanctification and righteousness. The rest of the verse says, "Seek and you will find. Knock and the door will be opened". To a Christian, this should mean – Ask, as a means to righteousness and holiness, and it will be given to you.

CONCLUSION - The conclusion of this analysis is self-evident. If the conclusion is not self-evident, then I can say no more.

MERCY – MATTHEW 16
Matthew 16:19-31

Jesus reveals so much to us in these verses about what He came to reveal to us. It starts off illustrating what God reveals most – mercy, or the lack of it. It continues by illustrating our eternal consequences – heaven or hell. Let us analyze what Jesus revealed in this passage.

(19) "There was a rich man who was dressed in purple and fine linen and lived in luxury every day. (20)At his gate was laid a beggar named Lazarus, covered with sores, (21)and longing to eat what fell from the rich man's table. Even the dogs came and licked his sores. (22)The time came when the beggar died, and the angels carried him to Abraham's side. The rich man also died and was buried.(23)In Hades, where he was in torment, he looked up and saw Abraham far away, with Lazarus at his side. (24)So he called to him, 'Father Abraham, have pity on me and send Lazarus to dip the tip of his finger in water and cool my tongue, because I am in agony in this fire'.

(25)"But Abraham replied, 'Son, remember that in your lifetime you received your good things, while Lazarus received bad things, but now he is comforted here and you are in agony. (26)And besides all this, between us and you a great chasm has been set in place, so that those who want to go from here to you cannot, nor can anyone cross over from there to us. (27)He answered, 'Then I beg you, father, send Lazarus to my family, (28)for I have five brothers. Let him warn them, so that they will not also come to this place of torment'.

(29)"Abraham replied, 'They have Moses and the prophets; let them listen to them'. (30)No, father Abraham', he said, 'but if someone from the dead goes to them, they will repent. (31)He said to him, 'If they do not listen to Moses and the Prophets, they will not be convinced even if someone rises from the dead'".

A Discussion of these verses:

Verse 19 – "There was a rich man who was dressed in purple and fine linen and lived in luxury every day".

Jesus describes a man who was fortunate to absorb all of the comforts of this world, but ignored the purpose of his affluence, and that was to use this affluence to go out into this world to show mercy and kindness to the less fortunate in His name.

Verses 20,21 – "At his gate was laid a beggar named Lazarus, covered with sores and longing to eat what fell from the rich man's table. Even the dogs came and licked his sores".

Lazarus was a man of many afflictions but who needed help and mercy. Lazarus sat at the feet of the rich man. The rich man made an obvious choice to ignore his suffering. This is the case of so many who have been given so much. They horde and absorb all the blessings of God. They do not use the blessings from God for their intended purpose. The purpose is to be the hands and feet of God and to show God's love and mercy to the least of these in the name of Jesus.

Verse 22 – "The time came when the beggar died, and the angels carried him to Abraham's side. The rich man also died and was buried".

Now the event takes a sudden turn. They both die. Lazarus is taken into heaven and sits in total security and comfort and total joy. The rich man is buried and goes to eternal punishment – hello! Note: the scripture does not discuss why the rich man went to hell. Did the rich man kill someone? Did he steal from someone or rob someone? No, none of these describe why. The scriptures only describe one sin – He did not show mercy. Mercy!! Jesus cares about mercy. He came to show us how to give mercy.

Verse 23 –"In Hades, where he was in torment, he looked up and saw Abraham far away, with Lazarus by his side".

In hell, the rich man was in torment – torment so bad that our minds cannot conceive of it. We cannot imagine what that kind of torment is. In addition to the torment of his body, he realizes another torment. He could have been where Lazarus was in the lap of Abraham. Note: When we die, the judgment is made – heaven or hell. Are you ready for the judgment? Remember, there are no second chances.

Verse 24 – "So he called to him, 'Father Abraham, have pity on me and send Lazarus to dip the tip of his finger in water and cool my tongue, because I am in agony in this fire".

Can we even begin to understand the eternal pain and agony of hell? The rich man who had so much comfort and did not use it to comfort Lazarus was asking for only one drop of water to relieve his agony. (There has to be a lesson in this passage for us). "I am in agony in this fire". Wow! Agony! The rich man will be in agony for eternity. We are given an opportunity to make a choice while we are living. When we die, the results of our decision are eternally put into action.

Verse 25 – "But Abraham replied, 'Son, remember that in your lifetime you received your good things while Lazarus received bad things, but now he is comforted here and you are in agony'."

Abraham's reply, "So, remember in your lifetime". The key word is "remember". There will be a time when you will have an accounting of your life. Big question – Are you ready for that?

Verse 26 – "And besides all this, between us and you a great chasm has been set in place, so that those who want to go from here to you cannot, nor can anyone cross over from there to us."

God describes a chasm between heaven and hell that cannot be breached. Those in heaven cannot go to hell and those in hell cannot go to heaven. That chasm between heaven and hell was created by sin – yes, SIN. In the Garden of Eden, God and Adam walked side by side – no chasm. When Adam sinned, God separated Himself from Adam, which transferred to all of his descendents.

Verses 27, 28 – "He answered, 'Then I beg you, father, send Lazarus to my family, (28)for I have five brothers. Let him warn them, so that they will not also come to this place of torment".

The rich man in hell realized his fate and then begs father Abraham to send Lazarus to warn his brothers of the consequences of sin so they may escape the same torment he is in. A very important thing is going on here. He now understands the value of mercy. He did not want his brothers to go through what he was going through. His torment could have been avoided if he had shown mercy before he died. Now he understands the cost of his sin and does not want his brothers to commit sin.

Verse 29 – "Abraham replied, 'They have Moses and the prophets; let them listen to them'.

God said they had Moses and the prophets and they did not listen. God sent Jesus, and we did not listen. Here is the message for today: God sent Jesus to pay the blood price to forgive our sin. We who are Christians are sent out unto the world to show God's mercy and to present the gospel of salvation. If we do not do that and keep our salvation to ourselves, we could be sitting in heaven watching our brothers and sisters in hell begging for a drop of water to cool their tongue. Note: Maybe all of the lost in hell will be crying out to you asking "why did you <u>not</u> tell me about Jesus and His salvation"?. Maybe the hardest question to answer will come from Jesus- Why did you <u>not</u> go out unto the world like I commanded you to do. Jesus talked more about going out unto the world in His name than any other subject.

Verses 30,31 – " 'No, father Abraham, he said,' but if someone from the dead goes to them, they will repent.' (31)He said to him, 'If they do not listen to Moses and the Prophets, they will not be convinced even if someone rises from the dead'."

This is prophetic. The rich man said, "But if someone from the dead go to them, they will repent". God is saying that His Son did rise from the dead and lives today, but people still do not listen. Oh, how I wish the lost would come to know Jesus.

Now, what can we learn from this?

1. This is not an illustration or parable. Read the first words of verse 19 – "There <u>was</u> a rich man". Jesus said "There was" which means this <u>was</u> an actual situation.
2. God is serious about "to whom much is given, much is expected". If you are given much, it is given to you to show <u>mercy</u>. Much is given to a few to show mercy for a lot. It is not given to you to elevate yourself over other people.

3. Hell is a real place – not a state of mind. The worst time to find out that it is real place is when you are in hell – for eternity.
4. Lazarus could see the rich man in hell. What if you could see a family member or friends in hell? What if they were begging you for one drop of water to cool their tongue? It would be torture to me to see a family member or friend or another person there, knowing that I never showed them the way to salvation.

Salvation is at hand today. Hell is at hand today. Are you ready for eternity?

NARROW IS THE GATE THAT LEADS TO LIFE
Matthew 7:13

"Enter through the narrow gate. For wide is the gate and broad is the road that leads to destruction, and many enter through it."

This is a shocking reality. The gate is narrow and not as wide as people would want it to be. Just by the nature of this statement, Jesus put some exact and well-defined conditions that made the gate narrow. It also means that there are perceptions created by man that would make the gate seem to be wide with few conditions to enter. But, there are conditions. Number one is you must be born again. Number two is based on a love for Him. If you do not love Him, how can you go to His dwelling place – heaven? So Jesus said in John 14:15, "If you love me, you will obey my commands". Since Jesus said that, the question is: What are His commands? These commands are detailed in the book Something to Consider. If these conditions exist, then what are the conditions to enter the narrow gate? Don't you think you should know what Jesus meant when He said "If you love me"? There is also a section in that same book <u>Something to Consider</u>, authored by David Leatherman. The section is titled "What Could Anger Jesus?" That also helps to define what makes the gate narrow. Jesus said that the gate is narrow. That statement carries eternal ramifications. AGAIN – Jesus made a declaration about the narrow gate in Matthew 20:1-16:

> "For the kingdom of heaven is like a landowner who went out early in the morning to hire men to work in his vineyard. He agreed to pay them a denarius for the day and sent them into his vineyard.

> "About the third hour he went out and saw others standing in the marketplace doing nothing. He told them, 'You also go and work in my vineyard and I will pay you whatever is right'. So they went.

> "He went out again about the sixth hour and the ninth hour and did the same thing. About the eleventh hour, he went out and found still others standing around. He asked them, 'Why have you been standing here all day long doing nothing?' 'Because no one has hired us,' they answered. He said to them, 'You also go and work in my vineyard.'

> "When evening came, the owner of the vineyard said to his foreman, 'Call the workers and pay them their wages, beginning with the last ones hired and going on to the first'. The workers who were hired about the eleventh hour came and each received a denarius.

"So when those came who were hired first, they expected to receive more. But each one of them also received a denarius. When they received it, they began to grumble against the landowner. 'These men who were hired last worked only one hour.' They said, 'and you have made them equal to us who have borne the burden of the work and the heat of the day.

"But he answered one of them, 'Friend, I am not being unfair to you. Didn't you agree to work for a denarius? Take what is yours and go your way. I wish to give to this last man the same as to you. Is it not lawful for me to do what I wish with my own things? Or is your eye evil because I am good?

"So the last will be first and the first last. For many are called, but few chosen."

Verse 16: "So the last will be first, and the first last. For many are called, but few chosen." Once again, Jesus is clearly stating that only a few are chosen which means the gate is narrow. I think that the chosen are the ones that really, really, really desire to love Him and serve His agenda, rather than the agendas of an organization or entity or self-interest.

People can seek Christ for a wide range of reasons. Once you get into the club of Christianity, those reasons can evolve into self-serving interests like: 1) a social meeting place, 2) a social meeting place of common interests, 3) in some places, like the South, a status symbol, 4) for business purposes, 5) a symbol of pride that shows up in the grandeur of the church buildings. The club of Christianity has a wide gate, but the narrow gate that leads to life is all about our heart's desire to serve God as shown by the example of His Son, Jesus

Christ. Jesus instructed us to go out into the world and be His voice and to show acts of kindness and mercy, to be teachers, preachers, missionaries, and doers of good works in His name. Jesus said certain believers will be blessed, which He described in the Beatitudes, Matthew 5:1-12:

> "Now when he saw the crowds, he went up on a mountainside and sat down. His disciples came to him, and he began to teach them saying:
>
> "Blessed are the poor in spirit, for theirs is the kingdom of heaven.
>
> Blessed are they that mourn, for they will be comforted.
>
> Blessed are the meek, for they will inherit the earth.
>
> Blessed are those who hunger and thirst for righteousness, for they will be filled.
>
> Blessed are the merciful, for they will be shown mercy.
>
> Blessed are the pure in heart, for they will see God.
>
> Blessed are the peacemakers, for they will be called sons of God.
>
> Blessed are those who are persecuted because of righteousness, for theirs is the kingdom of heaven.

Blessed are you when people insult you, persecute you and falsely say all kinds of evil
against you because of me. Rejoice and be glad,
because great is your reward in heaven, for in
the same way they persecuted the prophets
who were before you.

Now refer to Matthew 21:31-46. Jesus describes the nature
of His Bride, the church. He illustrates His workers as those
who go out into the world to fulfill His promise to the world.
Those who do His work are referred to as His "sheep". Those
who do not do His will are referred to as the "goats". What is
the eternal judgment of the sheep and goats? Check it out –
Matthew 25:44-46;

"They also will answer, 'Lord when did we see you hungry
or thirsty or a stranger or needing clothes or sick or in prison,
and did not help you'? He will reply, 'I tell you the truth; whatever you did not do for one of the least of these, you did not
do for me'. Then they will go away to eternal punishment, but
the righteous to eternal life".

I may not know a lot about a lot of things, but there is one
thing I know for sure. I DO NOT WANT TO BE THE GOAT Jesus
is referring to!

Jesus said the gate (the Christian belief system) is wide, but
the gate to eternal life is narrow. Note: Search yourself constantly as to why you want to pursue a Christian life. Is it to
serve God or to use God to serve you?

Remember, the standard that determines eternal judgment are not a person's standard, not a church's standard,
not a preacher's standard, but only God's standard set forth
in His bible.

OMISSION VS. COMMISSION

It is interesting to study the life of Jesus and to see how He reacted to the sins of omission and commission. It gives us a sense of His priority of each sin group. Sin can probably be broken down into two broad groups, or categories: the sin of commission or the sin of omission.

Commission – Acting contrary to what God defines as righteous behavior.

Example – stealing, gossiping, murmuring, etc.

Omission –Acting contrary to the way God wants us to respond by not doing what he has commanded us to do as His ambassadors. Example – The Great Commission (go into the world). Utilizing the gifts He has given for His glory, instead of our glory. Using those gifts to show the saved and unsaved the love and compassion He shows to us, also demonstrating the two fundamental principals He showed us what would unify and harmonize all relationships between all people – TO GIVE AND FORGIVE. If we study the life of Jesus, we can glean a glimpse of His heart on this subject.

THE WOMAN TAKEN IN ADULTERY – John 8:3-11

"The teachers of the law and the Pharisees brought in a woman caught in adultery. They made her stand before the group and said to Jesus, 'Teacher, this woman was caught in the act of adultery. In the Law, Moses commanded us to stone such women. Now what do you say?' They were using this question as a trap, in order to have a basis for accusing him."But Jesus bent and started to write on the ground with his finger. When they kept on questioning him, he straightened up and said to them, 'If any one of you is without sin, let him be the first to throw a stone at her.' Again, he stooped down and wrote on the ground."At this, those who heard began to go away one at a time, the older ones first, until only Jesus was left with the woman standing there. Jesus straightened up and asked her, 'Woman, where are they? Has no one condemned you?' 'No one, sir,' she said. "Then neither do I condemn you', Jesus declared. 'Go now and leave your life of sin.'"

Notice that Jesus recognized her sin (a sin of commission) and told her to go and sin no more (He forgave her). The self-proclaimed righteous leaders did not forgive her. They were in the sin of omission. They disobeyed the fundamentals of mercy Jesus came to teach us. The religious men should have forgiven her since God provided a way to cover their sins and they should have given her a chance to repent of her sins, since God did that for them. God showed mercy on them. Their sin of omission was to omit showing the woman the same mercy God had shown to them.

Another prime example of how Jesus viewed the sins of commission and omission is written in Matthew 23:1-36. Verse 23 says: "Woe to you, teachers of the law and Pharisees, you hypocrites! You give a tenth of your spices – mint, dill and cumin. But you have neglected the most important matters of the law – justice, mercy and faithfulness. You should have practiced the latter, without neglecting the former".

Notice that the Pharisees put a great emphasis on giving to the institution of the church. They considered it a <u>commission</u> of sin if they did not tithe, but actually committed the sin of <u>omission</u> by omitting the acts of justice, mercy and faith. Jesus considered the sin of <u>omission</u> to be a much greater sin than the sin of <u>commission</u>.

There are probably over 100 illustrations of how Jesus felt about the sins of commission and omission. My personal conclusion is that the <u>sin of omission </u>bothered Jesus more than the sin of commission. Jesus forgave all sin freely but seemed angered in most cases with the sin of omission. Consider the reaction of Jesus in Matthew 25 where He illustrates taking care of, or not taking care of, the least of His people (the sheep and the goats). Jesus seemed to be angered because they omitted mercy and compassion. Following is Matthew 25:42-46:

> "For I was hungry and you gave me nothing to eat. I was thirsty and you gave me nothing to drink. I was a stranger and you did not invite me in. I needed clothes and you did not clothe me. I was sick and in prison and you did not look after me. They also will answer, 'Lord, when did we see you hungry or thirsty or a stranger, or needing clothes, or sick or in prison and did not help you?' He will reply, 'I tell you the truth, whatever you did not do for one of the least of these, you did not do it for me'. Then they will go away to eternal punishment, but the righteous to eternal life'."

Look again at His reaction in verse 46 – "THEN THEY WILL GO AWAY TO ETERNAL PUNISHMENT, BUT THE RIGHTEOUS TO ETERNAL LIFE."

So what is the point of all that has been written? This is important – Jesus came to provide the blood price of our sin (Hebrews 9 and 10). He also came to replace all of the prophets and specially appointed people and priests who were intercessors between men and God. God appointed Jesus to be the only intercessor and appointed man to communicate His standard of righteousness through what God taught us through His Son Jesus. Man is now appointed to tell the world all that he wants the world to know about His plan, His love and his standard of righteousness. We are now His communicators and ambassadors. Jesus came to proclaim the new way and the new covenant between God and man. The old covenant was to concur by force and the new covenant is all about concurring by love through giving and forgiving. Jesus replaced all of the prophets (Moses, Elijah, etc.) and has commissioned each of us to go out into the world to be His hands, feet and mouth. He has given each of us very special gifts that are to be used to express His love for His people. Jesus has also given the last truth that will ever be given to man. Jesus expressed that truth though His holy scriptures – the Bible. NOW, we are commanded to be His ambassadors. It would be a serious sin of omission if we do not do that.

Jesus' last prayers before He went to the Garden of Gethsemane are written out in John 17. Think about it; this is His last prayer for Himself and for His disciples. Just think of the passion behind the prayer. In verses 1-5, Jesus prays for Himself. In verses 6-19, Jesus prays for His disciples (we are now His disciples).Notice verses 6-8:

> "I have revealed you to those whom you gave me out of the world. They were yours; you gave them to me and they have obeyed your word. Now they know that everything you have given me comes from you. For I gave them the words you gave me, and they accepted them. They knew with certainty that I came from you and they believed that you sent me."

Essentially, Jesus said – God, as much as you have given to me, I have given to them. My disciples are prepared. THEN, Jesus said in John 17:18 – "As you sent me into the world, I have sent them into the world." WOW. Jesus died to give us eternal life through His shed blood. Before He died, He commanded his disciples to go into the world. WOW. We are commissioned and commanded to be His ambassadors and to go into the world. It is my opinion that... if you really, really, really love Jesus, you have to take this seriously. When we die and stand at the judgment seat, it may come down to this: Did you do what Jesus commanded you to do?

My question is this: Are we prepared; are we committed; are we willing and, most of all are we doing what we are commanded to do? I personally believe that at judgment day, we will have to answer more questions about our sins of <u>omission</u> than the sins of <u>commission</u>. It seems to me that He forgives the sins of <u>commission</u> but He seems to be more disturbed by the sins of <u>omission.</u>

What are your thoughts on this subject? It is a highly important subject.

ON THIS ROCK I WILL BUILD MY CHURCH
Matthew 16:13-19
(Special attention to verses 17 and 18)

(13) "When Jesus came to the region of Caesarea Philippi, he asked his disciples, 'Who do you say the Son of Man is?' (14) They replied 'Some say John the Baptist; others say Elijah and still others, Jeremiah or one of the prophets. (15) 'But what about you?' he asked. 'Who do you say I am?' (16) Simon Peter answered, 'You are the Christ, the Son of the living God.' (17) Jesus replied, 'Blessed are you, Simon, son of Jonah, for this was not revealed to you by man, but by my Father in heaven. (18) And I tell you that you are Peter, and on this rock I will build my church, and the gates of hell will not overcome it. (19) I will give you the keys of the kingdom of heaven; whatever you bind on earth will be

bound in heaven, and whatever you loose on earth will be loosed in heaven.'"

It is interesting that volumes of books have been written on what Jesus meant when he referred to "this rock". There have been religious systems built on what Jesus meant when He referred to the "rock" and His church, because the premise of the "rock" becomes the basis of their doctrine, a method of justification for their religious system.

As for me, the meaning Jesus was referring to is very clear and clearly lines up with the intent and purpose of what Jesus came to earth for. Jesus came to earth to reveal His Father's truth to mankind. Several passages in scripture make reference to the "rock". All of these passages lead back to Jesus as being the Rock. The book of John, Chapter 1:1, 14 – "In the beginning was the Word, and the Word was with God, and the Word was God. He was with God in the beginning. The Word became flesh and made his dwelling among us. We have seen his glory, the glory of the One and Only, who came from the Father, full of grace and truth."

God's truth was His Word and God said His truth, "His Word", became flesh. His truth came in the flesh of Jesus Christ. Now, God is going to build His church on His truth, the Word that became flesh – "Jesus". There are several passages that specifically talk about Jesus being the Rock. Two examples are:

I Cor. 10:4 – "and drank the same spiritual drink for they drank from the spiritual rock that accompanied them, and that rock was Christ."

Deuteronomy 32:4 – "He is the Rock; his works are perfect and all his ways are just."

Yes, it is very clear, actually, crystal clear that the truth of God, which is Jesus, is the Rock He is building His church on.

Truth #1 – Jesus asked the disciples, "Who do you say that I am?" Peter answered, "You are the Christ, the Son of the living God." Jesus' response to that was "...for this was not revealed to you by man, but by my Father in heaven." Peter said, "You are the Christ, the Son of the Living God." This is the Rock that Jesus was referring to that God would build His church on – "For this was not revealed to you by man, but by my Father in heaven," and "You are the Christ, the Son of the living God." God would personally reveal His truth to man and would do it through His son, Jesus Christ. Jesus went on to confirm to Peter that He is the Christ. Jesus was appointed to be the messenger for His Father to reveal the divine truth from God, the Father. This truth would be the basis of God's relationship to man. That truth is this: God will reveal to us what he wants us to know. Man cannot reveal any of God's truth except by the only truth revealed through Jesus Christ, which is revealed in the Holy Scriptures. The reference to the rock is the principal and substance of His church, especially when you come to understand the entire purpose of Jesus, the Christ. The purpose of Jesus, the Christ, was to deliver the message that God sent Him to reveal. Jesus came to reveal the truth of God and the fact that God WILL REVEAL HIS TRUTH TO MAN. Man, apart from God, has no divine truth. This is the message of the New Covenant given by Jesus.

The fact that God sent Jesus to establish His church on the basis that God reveals His truth to man is prevalent throughout the New Testament. I can think of two places in the Bible that are especially meaningful to me and will be pointed out and discussed later. As clear as this is to understand, there are other church entities that have defined Peter as the "rock" of God's church. These churches claim Peter is the tool of revelation and appoints him to intercede on God's behalf, to reveal God's truth and divine purpose of God's plan for humanity. One particular religious entity (which is one of the largest church entities in the world) appointed Peter as the first Pope and bestowed upon him what is termed as infallible powers, meaning Peter was without sin and had exclusive rights to interpret God's scripture and intentions for humanity. This same religious entity went on to appoint Peter as the high priest. Peter was also appointed the title of "Father". All of the Popes to follow Peter were also appointed as "Father" and the High Priest. These appointments to infallibility, High Priest, and Father all contradict the Scriptures.

Now, consider the life of Peter to see if he would meet the criteria to be the rock/Pope which requires infallibility set by the standards of the church. Peter appeared to be <u>weak</u> because he denied Jesus at His moment of great need; not only that, but he <u>lied</u> when he denied Jesus because just moments before he said he would not deny Him. <u>Satan</u>! Jesus referred to Peter as "<u>Satan</u>" – verse 23. That does not sound like someone to fill the role of Pope or to be the rock as it is defined. <u>Impetuous</u>! Peter reacted before thinking in many cases. That is a sign of instability. <u>Trustworthiness</u>! While Jesus was in the Garden of Gethsemane agonizing about his fate, Peter fell asleep – Matthew 26:40. <u>Commitment</u>! Jesus showed Himself to Peter again at the Sea of Tiberius after His resurrection. After all that Peter had seen and experienced, and even after the great commission to go unto the world, Jesus found Peter back into the world that he came from – fishing for fish instead of fishing for men – John 21:15-19. <u>Given all of this, and more, why would Peter be appointed the rock</u> that Jesus would build his church on? I still contend that the rock is the response that Jesus gave to Peter – "For this was not revealed to you by man, but by my Father in Heaven". This is the infallible rock that he was going to build his church on. God's revelation to man and that revelation is His Holy Bible which was given to us through the life of His Son, Jesus Christ.

Question: How is this contrary to the Scriptures? Answer: Infallibility – SIN – ALL men are born in sin and will be sinful

until death says the Scriptures. No man is infallible to sin –
Romans 5:12. - (12)

> "When Adam sinned, sin entered the entire
> human race. His sin spread death through all
> the world, so everything began to grow old and
> die, for all sinned."

High Priest – To further clarify the position of High Priest,
consider Hebrews 8:1-5:

> (1) "The point of what we are saying is this:
> We do have such a high priest who sat down
> at the right hand of the throne of the Majesty
> in heaven (2) and who serves in the sanctuary,
> the true tabernacle set up by the Lord, not by
> man. (3) Every high priest is appointed to offer
> both gifts and sacrifices and so it was necessary
> for this one to have something to offer. (4) If
> he were on earth, he would not be a priest, for
> there are already men who offer the gifts pre-
> scribed by law. They serve at a sanctuary that is
> copy and shadow of what is in heaven. (5) This
> is why Moses was warned when he was about
> to build the tabernacle, 'See to it that you make
> everything according to the pattern shown to
> you on the mountain.' "

These and other Scriptures clearly appoint Jesus as the only
Priest, or High Priest over man. Jesus is the author and inter-
preter of God's truth given to man, not an earthly man. The
truth revealed to men through Jesus is the basis of His church.

Father – The name Father carries with it an extreme
authority and responsibility to care for and protect his family.
In a spiritual sense, the name Father is only to be used in

reference to our heavenly Father. He, and only He, has the authority and responsibility to care for our spiritual need. In an earthly sense, father is used as head of the household with the same authority and responsibility to care for his family.

> Matthew 23:9 – "And do not call any man on earth 'father', for you have one Father, and He is in heaven."

Further, in this essay, you will read about the prayer Jesus had just prior to going to the Garden of Gethsemane just before his death. What Jesus is essentially praying is "I have done what you sent me to do. I have given to all humanity all the knowledge and divine revelation that you have given to me and now I send them out into the world to do your work." What this means is, the Priesthood is not needed nor is it wanted. Peter is not the priesthood or the rock God built His church on, neither are any of the churches (man based) appointed church leaders or Popes. The Holy Spirit within each of us is God's direct communication with each of us. God has truth and revelation for each one of us and that truth and revelation comes by the way of God's Scripture and through an intimate prayerful relationship with God through Jesus. Our Holy Spirit guides us by that truth.

Truth #2 - Revelation from God. The last and complete Truth came to all humanity through Jesus the Christ. Jesus said, "I have given them all that you have sent me to give them." This truth has been recorded and is known as the Holy Bible. THIS IS THE ROCK THAT JESUS WAS REFERRING TO. The Scriptures go on to say that the revelation of this truth is buried within our soul in the form of the Holy Spirit (God within us). The nurturing of this truth comes from study and prayer.

I mentioned earlier that there are many places in the Bible that discuss the revelation of God and His truth, but there are two particular places that are meaningful to me – John 17:6-19 and Hebrews 8.

John 17:6-19 – Jesus prays for His disciples before entering the Garden of Gethsemane - (6) "I have revealed to those whom you gave me out of the world. They were yours; you gave them to me and they have obeyed your word. (7) Now they know that everything you have given me comes from you. (8) For I gave them the words you gave me and they accepted them. They knew with certainty that I came from you and they believed that you sent me. (9) I pray for them. I am not praying for the world, but for those you have given me, for they are yours. (10) All I have is yours and all you have is mine. And glory has come to me through them. (11) I will remain in the world no longer, but they are still in the world and I am coming to you. Holy Father, protect them by the power of your name. – the name you gave me – so that they may be one as we are one. (12) While I was with them, I protected them and kept them safe by the name you gave me. None has been lost except one doomed to destruction so that Scripture would be fulfilled.

(13) I am coming to you now, but I say these things while I am still in the world, so that they may have the full measure of my joy within them. (14) I have given them your word and the world has hated them, for they are not of the world any more than I am of the world. (15) My prayer is not that you take them out of this

> world, but that you protect them from the evil
> one. (16) They are not of the world, even as I
> am not of it. (17) Sanctify them by the truth;
> your word is truth. (18) As you sent me into the
> world, I have sent them into the world. (19) For
> them I sanctify myself, that they too may be
> truly sanctified.

Jesus prays for our protection AND SENDS US OUT INTO THE WORLD. WOW! Please read these verses over and over again. There is so much more about these verses that can be written than this short essay has space for. The two vital messages that come from God through the Scriptures are these: HE LOVES US BEYOND ANY POSSIBLE MEASURE AND SENT HIS SON TO DIE ON THE CROSS FOR REDEMPTION OF OUR SIN. The other message is this: HIS CHURCH WILL BE BUILT ON GOD'S TRUTH GIVEN TO MAN. ALSO HIS CHURCH WILL <u>NOT</u> BE BUILT ON A SINFUL MAN APPOINTED AS HIGH PRIEST BY OTHER SINFUL MEN.

John 17:20-26 – Jesus prays for all believers -

(20) "My prayer is not for them alone. I pray also for those will believe in me through their message; (21) that all of them may be one, Father, just as you are in me and I am in you. May they also be in us so that the world may believe that you have sent me. (22) I have given them the glory that you gave me, that they may be one as we are one. (23) I in them, and you in me. May they be brought to complete unity to let the world know that you sent me and have loved them even as you have loved me."

> (24) "Father, I want those you have given me
> to be with me where I am, and to see my glory,
> the glory you have given me because you loved
> me before the creation of the world."

(25) "Righteous Father, though the world does not know you, I know you and they know that you have sent me. (26) I have made you known to them, and I will continue to make you known in order that the love you have for me may be in them and that I myself may be in them."

WOW! Jesus prayed for us just before He surrendered His life for us. Please read these Scriptures a hundred times or more. This prayer that Jesus gave is for us, his ambassadors. Jesus loves us so much. Notice verse 21: - "...that all of them may be one, Father, just as you are in me, and I am in you. May they also be in us so that the world may believe that you have sent me."

Jesus prayed that God, the Father, and He himself, the Christ, and we would be as one. Read Verse 22 - "I have given them the glory that you gave me, that they may be one as we are one."

Jesus said, "Give them the glory that you gave me." Think about what Jesus said, "Give them the Glory (the glory) you gave me." What could be greater than that? This has got to be the most intimate prayer given for His followers.

The other Scripture that is meaningful to me is Hebrews 8:1-13, with particular attention to verses 7-13:

(1) "The point of what we are saying is this: We do have such a high priest who sat down at the right hand of the throne of the Majesty in heaven (2) and who serves in the sanctuary, the true tabernacle set up by the Lord, not by man.

(3)"Every high priest is appointed to offer both gifts and sacrifices, and so it was necessary for this one also to have something to offer. (4) If he were on earth, he would not be a priest, for there are already men who offer the gifts prescribed by the law. (5) They serve at a sanctuary that is a copy and shadow of what is in heaven. This is why Moses was warned when he was about to build the tabernacle: 'See to it that you make everything according to the pattern shown you on the mountain'. (6) But the ministry Jesus has received is as superior to theirs as the covenant of which he is mediator is superior to the old one, and it is founded on better promises.

(7) For if there had been nothing wrong with that first covenant, no place would have been sought for another. (8) But God found fault with the people and said: 'The time is coming', declares the Lord, 'when I will make a new covenant with the house of Israel and with the house of Judah. (9) It will not be like the covenant I made with their forefathers when I took them by the hand to lead them out of Egypt because they did not remain faithful to my covenant and I turned away from them', declares the Lord. (10) This is the covenant I will make in the house of Israel after I put my laws in their minds and write them on their hearts. I will be their God and they will be my people.

(11) No longer will a man teach his neighbor or a man his brother, saying, 'Know the Lord,' because they will all know me, from the least of them to the greatest. (12) For I will forgive their wickedness and will remember their sins no more.

(13) By calling this covenant 'new', he has made the first one obsolete, and what is obsolete and aging will soon disappear."

These verses clearly define that God's revelations to man come from God and <u>not</u> through an earthly, sinful man. Therefore, these verses would naturally, by logic and presumption, indicate that the "rock" that God's church would be built upon would be God's revelation to man, not man's revelation to himself. Notice verses 10-12 -

(10) "This is the covenant I will make with the house of Israel after that time, declares the Lord. I will put my laws in their minds and write them on their hearts. I will be their God, and they will be my people. (11) No longer will a man teach his neighbor or a man his brother, 'Know the Lord', because they will all know me, from the least of them to the greatest. (12) For I will forgive their wickedness and will remember their sins no more."

NEW COVENANT – Read Verse 13: - "By calling this covenant 'new', he had made the first one obsolete, and what is obsolete and aging will soon disappear."

We are under a new covenant which was given to us through Jesus Christ. This subject (the New Covenant) is very extensive and yet so simple. To do this study justice, it would require a separate essay. This subject of "The New Covenant" is discussed in the book <u>Something to Consider</u>, of which I am the author.

Hopefully, this subject has value to you. The book of Hebrews is a fascinating book. Chapters 8,9,10 and 11 are full of God's purpose, the purpose of Jesus, the nature of God's creation, the passion of God and His love for His people.

One last fact that needs to be established – Jesus was sent to earth in a carnal form to live among the people in the flesh to establish God's standards of righteousness so that those standards of righteousness were the purest form of love that man could show to God and to all fellowmen. If man would live by these standards of righteousness, then man could live in total harmony. Most of those standards can be condensed down to three properties or attributes. Man must do three things – give, forgive and to show mercy to one another. WOW! The other purpose of Jesus was coming to earth to satisfy the first covenant/law given to man. That first covenant/law was called the "Blood Covenant".

The Blood Covenant – Hebrews Chapter 9:
Verse 18 –
"This is why even the first covenant was not put into effect without blood".
Verses 19 -20 –
"When Moses had proclaimed every commandment of the law to all the people, he took the blood of calves together with water, scarlet wool and branches of hyssop and sprinkled the scroll and all the people. He said, 'This is the blood of the covenant, which God has commanded you to keep.' "
Verse 22 –
"In fact, the law required that nearly everything be cleansed with blood, and without the shedding of blood, there is no sacrifice for sin."

Because of the sin of Adam and Eve, man was born with a dirty heart of sin. Before man could approach God, that dirty sin had to cleansed with innocent blood, as required by God. Jesus came to provide the innocent blood to cleanse man of his sin so that man could be presentable to God. Thank you God and Jesus for that incredible gift - Jesus would sacrifice His life to satisfy the blood covenant. Thank you again.

Now, here are two more scriptures that support my conclusions about what and who the rock is: Old Testament – Deuteronomy 32:3,4 –

"I will proclaim the name of the LORD. O praise the Greatness of our God! He is the Rock; his works are perfect, and all his ways are just."

New Testament – I Corinthians 10:3 –

"They all ate the same spiritual food and drank the same spiritual drink; for they drank from the rock that accompanied them, and that rock was Christ."

MISSION WORK AND GOD'S CALL FOR AMBASSADORS

All of creation is justified by the first four words in the Bible: "IN THE BEGINNING GOD".

Question: Why does God want missionaries, ambassadors and churches?

A. History

1. God's creation and the Garden of Eden experience.

    a) God created all things, Genesis 1 and 2.
    b) God created man and woman, Genesis 1 and 2.
    c) God wanted to love and be loved, so He gave man an option to show or not show his love – the forbidden fruit, Genesis 2: 17-17.
    d) They knew their nakedness so God provided an animal skin for cover (first blood in the Garden of Eden would, forever, be the cost of a relationship with God). Hebrews 9, specifically verses 15 and 22.

e) God banished Adam and Eve from the Garden of Eden. Genesis 3:23, He guarded the way back in with a flaming sword. Genesis 3:24.

2. God changed His relationship with man.

   a) God separated Himself from man and would never DIRECTLY communicate with man except through a mediator (prophet), and sin would never be forgiven except through the giving of blood.
   b) Man desired and needed a relationship with his creator. That desire and need never went away. At birth, we are born of flesh and soul. The flesh desires freedom from God and our soul desires a relationship with God. Flesh – all about me. Soul – not about me but God.

3. Study the bible history of how God communicated with man.

   a) Abraham and Moses – God spoke to His people through Abraham and Moses.
   b) The Prophets – Daniel, Joseph, Habakkuk, Nehemiah, Solomon, David, Jeremiah, Isaiah, Malachi and many more. God did not communicate directly with man except through a human mediator. The Jewish faith still teaches this same principle and the Roman Catholic Church practices the same principle to a large extent since the Pope determines truth and none truth. Study the accounts of the prophets.

4. Man could not look upon God, Hebrews 9:1-10.

a) Atonement of sins – a priest, at a specific time and under specific conditions, could enter the Holy of Holies, the Ark of the Covenant, for atonement.
b) Moses, at Mt. Sinai, could not look upon God, only upon a burning bush.

B. Jesus became the mediator of the New Covenant. Hebrews 9:15. The Old Covenant relationship with man did not work. Hebrews 8, I Corinthians 10:4-3, Galatians 3:15-25, Hebrews 1:16. So:

1. In the Old Covenant, God had a duty relationship with man.

   a) God has all kinds of laws. He told man what to do, how to do it and when to do it. He conquered through strength and wars. He showed His majesty through Solomon's Temple.

2. In the New Covenant, God changed His relationship from duty driven to desire drive. Instead of conquering by might and wars, He conquers through love, giving, and forgiving.

3. God's relationship with man changed and so did His method of communicating with man.

   a) Abraham and Moses are dead. The prophets are dead, and there with be no more prophets.
   b) One method of God's communication with man is now through us, His chosen people. We are His actions and voice. We are His ambassadors, His evangelists, His kindness, His mercy, His hand and feet of good works, His teachers

of the standards of His righteousness and His example of giving and forgiving.

c) Another method of communication is through the bible. The bible is the last truth given to man. The bible, which is the word of God, is the sword that separates God's truth from Satan's lies. We must have the weapon (the sword of the Spirit) which is the Holy Bible to be part of our armor of protection.

d) Prayer is method of communication. The most intimate relationship with God you will ever have is through prayer. Your intimacy with God, your knowledge of God and His plans for your life is only as strong as your intimate prayer with him.

e) Lastly, the most important method of communication comes from within. After we accept Jesus as our Savior, the scripture says that the Holy Spirit enters in. As Jesus' time on earth came to a close, He told his disciples, "I have much more to say to you, more than you can now bear. But, when He, the spirit of truth comes, He will guide you into all truth. He will not speak on His own; He will speak only what He hears, and He will tell you what is yet to come." John 16:12-13; the bible also tells us that when we do not know what to pray, the Holy Spirit prays for us according to the **will of God.**

4. Jesus knew He was sent by His father to die on the cross for our sins, but He also knew that he was sent to establish God's standards of righteousness. He was sent to train people to communicate to man what His New Covenant was all about.

a) Disciples – God chose 12 disciples. The 12 disciples were a cross section of all four human temperaments and all of the economic lines and all of the social lines.

b) He spent three years teaching His disciples the standard of God's righteousness.

c) The disciples experienced miracles with Him: casting out demons, bringing the dead back to life, other healings and miracles.

d) The disciples saw Jesus challenge the religious leaders of the day.

e) The disciples watched Jesus weep and laugh with joy.

5. Jesus knew the time of the cross was near. He revealed himself clearly and they now knew with certainty the truth of His mission. Matthew 16:13-28 (Peter's confession).

   a) His disciples needed to be preparing to be disciplers, rather than disciples.

   b) His disciples needed to be teachers, ambassadors, missionaries, and church planters.

   c) Read Matthew 16:13-20 and 23-28.

6. The Holy Spirit – after the death and resurrection of Jesus, The Holy Spirit was breathed on man. Now God lives within us as our constant companion the Holy Spirit which always reminds us of what God wants us to do and what He does not want us to do.

   a) This is neat to me. After Adam and Eve sinned, man could not be in the presence of God or look upon God. God came to earth through His Son Jesus, and then man could see God, feel God and be in the presence of God. God stepped forward one more time and now dwells within man through the Holy Spirit.

7. God's Commission

    a) Mark 1:17 "Come and follow me, and I will make you fishers of men."
    b) The Great Commission – Mark 28:19-20 "Therefore, go and make disciples of all nations, baptizing them in the name of the Father and the Son and the Holy Spirit, teaching them to obey everything I have commanded you. And surely I am with you always, to the very end of the age."
    c) II Corinthians 5:10-11 "For we must all appear before the judgment seat of Christ, that each one may receive what is due him for the thing done while in the body, whether good or bad. Since then, we know what it is to fear the Lord, we try to persuade men."
    d) Ephesians 6:18-19 "And pray in the Spirit on all occasions, with all kinds of prayers and requests. With this in mind, be alert and always keep on praying for all the saints."
    e) The most compelling verses – Jesus in the Garden of Gethsemane. John 17:13-19; Jesus prays for His disciples. We are now His disciples.

8. Our commission is clear. We are the ambassadors, evangelists, missionaries, teachers, doers, and servants of the Lord. ARE YOU READY FOR THAT? Abraham is dead. Moses is dead. The prophets are dead. You are the living communicator for our living Lord.

a) Ephesians 6:19-20 – I am an ambassador.
b) II Corinthians 5:20 – We are therefore Christ's ambassadors.

OUR CALL TO THE MINISTRY

MARK 1:16,17 – JESUS WALKED BY THE SEA OF GALILEE AND MADE FISHERS OF MEN.

"As Jesus walked beside the Sea of Galilee, He saw Simon and his brother Andrew casting a net into the lake, for they were fishermen. 'Come, follow me', Jesus said, 'and I will make you fishers of men'."

MATTHEW 28:16-20 – THE GREAT COMMISSION

"Then the eleven disciples went to Galilee, to the mountain where Jesus had told them to go. When they saw Him they worshiped him, but some doubted. Then Jesus came to them and said, 'All authority in heaven and on earth has been given to me. Therefore, go and make disciples of all nations, baptizing them in the name of the Father and of the Son and of the Holy Spirit, teaching them to obey everything I have commanded you. And surely I will be with you always, to the very end of the age'."

MATTHEW 16:13-15: CAESAREA PHILIPPI – JESUS' CONFESSION

"When Jesus came to the region of Caesarea Philippi, he asked his disciples, 'who do people say the Son of Man is'? They replied, 'Some say John the Baptist, others say Elijah and still others, Jeremiah or one of the prophets.

'But what about you?', he asked. 'Who do you say I am?' Simon Peter answered, 'You are the Christ, the Son of the living God'. Jesus replied, 'Blessed are you Simon, son of Jonah, for this was not revealed to you by men, but by my Father in heaven. And I tell you that you are Peter, and on this rock I will build my church, and the gates of Hades will not overcome it. I will give you the keys of the kingdom of heaven; whatever you bind on earth will be bound in heaven, and whatever you loose on earth will be loosed in heaven'. Then he warned his disciples not to tell anyone that he was the Christ.

"From that time on, Jesus began to explain to His disciples that he must go to Jerusalem and suffer many things at the hands of the elders, chief priests and teachers of the law, and that he must be killed and on the third day be raised to life. Peter took him aside and began to rebuke him, 'Never Lord', he said. 'This shall never happen to you'. Jesus turned and said to Peter, 'Out of my sight, Satan. You are a stumbling block to me; you do not have in mind the things of God, but the things of men.

"Then Jesus said to his disciples, 'If anyone would come after me, he must deny himself and take up his cross and follow me. For whoever wants to save his life will lose it, but whoever loses his life for me will find it. What good will it be for a man if he gains the whole world yet forfeits his soul? Or what can a man give in exchange for his soul? For the Son of Man is going to come in His Father's glory with His angels, and then He will reward each person according to what he has done. I tell you the truth; some who are standing here will not taste death before they see the Son of Man coming into his kingdom'.

JOHN 15:13-17 – YOU ARE MY FRIEND. GO BEAR FRUIT.

"Greater love has no one than this that he lay down his life for his friends. You are my friends if you do what I command. I no longer call you servants, because a servant does not know his master's business. Instead, I have called you friends, for everything that I learned from my Father I have made known to you.

"You did not choose me, but I chose you and appointed you to go and bear fruit – fruit that will last. Then the Father will give you whatever you ask in my name. This is my command: Love each other."

JOHN 14:15-21 – THE WORLD WILL NOT SEE ME, BUT WILL SEE YOU.

"If you love me, you will obey what I command. And I will ask the Father, and he will give you another Counselor to be with you forever – the Spirit of truth. The world cannot accept him, because it neither sees him nor knows him. But you know him, for he lives with you and will be in you.

"I will not leave you as orphans; I will come to you. Before long, the world will not see me anymore, but you will see me. Because I live, you also will live. On that day you will realize that I am in my Father, and you are in me, and I am in you. Whoever has my commands and obeys them, he is the one who loves me. He who loves me will be loved by my Father, and I too will love him and show myself to him."

MARK 13:10 – SIGNS OF THE END TIMES – JESUS SAID

"And the gospel must be preached to all nations."

MATTHEW 25:31-46 – THE SHEEP AND THE GOATS – JESUS SAID

"When the Son of Man comes in his glory, and all the angels with him, he will sit down on his throne in heavenly glory. All the nations will be gathered before Him, and He will separate the people one from another as a shepherd separates the sheep from the goats. He will put the sheep on his right; the goats on his left. "The the King will say to those on his right, 'Come, you who are blessed by my Father; take your inheritance, the kingdom prepared for you since the creation of the world. For I was hungry and you have me something to eat. I was thirsty and you gave me something to drink. I was a stranger and you invited me in. I needed clothes, and you clothed me. I was sick and you looked after me. I was in prison and you came to visit me.

"Then the righteous will answer him, 'Lord, when did we see you hungry and feed you, or thirsty and gave you something to drink? When did we see you a stranger and invite you in or needing clothes and clothe you? When did we see you sick or in prison and go to visit you?' The King will reply, 'I tell you the truth; whatever you did for one of the least of these brothers of mine, you did it for me.

"Then he will say to those on his left, 'Depart from me, you who are cursed into the eternal fire prepared for the devil and his angels. For I was hungry and you gave me nothing to eat. I was thirsty and you gave me nothing to drink. I was a stranger and you did not invite me in. I needed clothes and you did not clothe me. I was sick and in prison and you did not look after me'. They also will answer, 'Lord, when did we see you hungry or thirsty or a stranger or needing clothes or sick or in prison and did not help you?' He will reply, 'I tell you the truth. Whatever you did not do for one of the least of these, you did not do for me'. Then they will go away to eternal punishment, but the righteous to eternal life."

MATTHEW 26:36-46 – JESUS WITH HIS DISCIPLES IN THE GARDEN OF GETHSEMANE. Note Luke 22:44.

"Then Jesus went with his disciples to a place called Gethsemane, and he said to them, 'Sit here while I go over there and pray'. He took Peter and the two sons of Zebedee along with him, and he began to be sorrowful and troubled. Then he said to them, 'My soul is overwhelmed with sorrow to the point of death. Stay here and keep watch with me'.

"Going a little farther, He fell with His face to the ground and prayed, 'My Father, if it is possible, may this cup be taken from me. Yet, not as I will, but as You will.' Then he returned to his disciples and found them sleeping. 'Could you men not keep watch with me for one hour?' he asked Peter. 'Watch and pray so that you will not fall into temptation. The spirit is willing, but the body is weak.'

"He went away for a second time and prayed, 'My Father, if it is not possible for this cup to be taken away unless I drink it, may Your will be done'. When he came back, he again found them sleeping, because their eyes were heavy. So he left them and went away once more and prayed the third, saying the same thing.

"Then he returned to his disciples and said to them, 'Are you still sleeping and resting? Look, the hour is near, and the Son of Man is betrayed into the hands of sinners. Rise; let us go! Here comes my betrayer!' "

JOHN 17:1-26 – JESUS PRAYS FOR HIMSELF, FOR HIS DISCIPLES AND ALL THOSE WHO WILL BELIEVE IN HIM.

"After Jesus said this, He looked toward heaven and prayed: 'Father, the time has come. Glorify Your Son that Your Son may glorify You. For You granted him authority over all people that he might give eternal life to all those You have given him. Now this is eternal life: that they may know You, the only true God, and Jesus Christ, whom You have sent. I have brought You glory on earth by completing the work You gave me to do. And now, Father, glorify me in Your presence with the glory I had with You before the world began.

'I have revealed You to those whom You gave me out of the world. They were Yours; You gave them to me, and they have obeyed Your word. Now they know that everything You have given me comes from You. For I gave them the words You gave me, and they accepted them. They knew with certainty that I came from You, and they believed that You sent me. I pray for them. I am not praying for the world, but for those you have given me, for they are Yours. All I have is Yours, and all You have is mine. And glory has come to me through them. I will remain in the world no longer, but they are still in the world, and I am coming to You. Holy Father, protect them by the power of Your name – the name You gave me – so that they may be one as we are one. While I was with them, I protected them and kept them safe by the name You gave me. None has been lost except the one doomed to destruction so that the Scripture would be fulfilled.

'I am coming to you now, but I say these things while I am still in the world, so that they may have the full measure of my joy within them. I have given them Your word and the world has hated them, for they are not of the world any more than I am of the world. My prayer is not that you take them out of the world but that you protect them from the evil one. They are not of the world, even as I am not of it. Sanctify them by the truth; Your word is truth. As you sent me into the world, I have sent them into the world. For them I sanctify myself that they too may be truly sanctified.

'My prayer is not for them alone. I pray also for those who will believe in me through their message, that all of them may be one, Father, just as You are in me and I am in You. May they also be in us so that the world may believe that You have sent me. I have given them the glory that You gave me, that they may be one as we are one. I in them and You in me. May they be brought to complete unity to let the world know that You sent me and have loved them even as You have loved me.

'Father, I want those You have given me to be with me where I am and to see my glory, the glory You have given me because You loved me before the creation of the world. Righteous Father, though the world does not know You, I know You, and they know that You have sent me. I have made You known to them and will continue to make You known in order that the love You have for me may be in them and that I myself may be in them'."

JOHN 21:15-23 – JESUS RETURNS; PETER, DO YOU LOVE ME?

"When they had finished eating, Jesus said to Simon Peter, 'Simon, son of John, do you truly love me more than these'? 'Yes, Lord', he said, 'you know that I love you.' Jesus said, 'Feed my lambs'.

"Again, Jesus said, 'Simon, son of John, do you truly love me?' He answered, 'Yes, Lord, you know that I love you'. Jesus said, 'Take care of my sheep'.

"The third time he said to him, 'Simon, son of John, do you love me?' Peter was hurt because Jesus asked him the third time, 'Do you love me?' He said, 'Lord, you know all things; you know that I love you'.

"Jesus said, 'Feed my sheep. I tell you the truth; when you were younger you dressed yourself and went where you wanted, but when you are old, you will stretch out your hands, and someone else will dress you and lead you where you do not want to go'. Jesus said this to indicate the kind of death by which Peter would glorify God. Then he said to him, 'Follow me'. "Peter turned and saw that the disciple whom Jesus loved was following them. (This was the one who had leaned back against Jesus at the supper and had said, 'Lord, who is going to betray you'?) When Peter saw him, he asked 'Lord, what about him?' Jesus answered, 'If I want him to remain alive until I return, what is that to you? You must follow me'. Because of this, the rumor spread among the brothers that this disciple would not die. But Jesus did not say that he would not die; he only said, 'If I want him to remain alive until I return, what is that to you'?

"This is the disciple who testifies to these things and who wrote them down. We know that his testimony is true".

"Jesus did many other things as well. If every one of them were written down, I suppose that even the whole world would not have room for the books that would be written".

LUKE 24:45-49 – JUST BEFORE THE ASCENSION, JESUS REVEALS REPENTANCE AND FORGIVENESS

"Then he opened their minds so they could understand the Scriptures. He told them, 'This is what is written: The Christ will suffer and rise from the dead on the third day, and repentance and forgiveness of sins will be preached in his name to all nations, beginning at Jerusalem. You are witnesses of these things. I am going to send you what my Father has promised, but stay in the city until you have been clothed with power from on high'."

II CORINTHIANS 2:17 – WE DO NOT PEDDLE THE WORD OF GOD FOR PROFIT.

"Unlike so many, we do not peddle the word of God for profit. On the contrary, in Christ we speak before God with sincerity, like men sent from God."

"He has made us competent as ministers of a new covenant – not of the letter but of the Spirit; for the letter kills, but the Spirit gives life".

EVANGELISM SCRIPTURES:

MARK 16:15 – GO INTO ALL THE WORLD –

"He said to them, 'Go into all the world and preach the gospel to all creation'."

MATTHEW 28:19 - MAKE DISCIPLES OF ALL NATIONS –

"Therefore, go and make disciples of all nations, baptizing them in the name of the Father and of the Son and of the Holy Spirit".

ACTS 1:8 – BE MY WITNESSES TO THE END OF THE EARTH –

"But you will receive power when the Holy Spirit comes on you, and you will be my witnesses in Jerusalem, and in all Judea and Samaria, and to the ends of the earth."

MATTHEW 9:37, 38 – SEND OUT WORKERS INTO HIS HARVEST FIELD -

"Then he said to his disciples, 'The harvest is plentiful but the workers are few. Ask the Lord of the harvest, therefore, to send out workers into his harvest field."

ROMANS 10:11-15 - PREACH SO THAT THEY CAN KNOW GOD. –

"How then can they call on the one they have not believed in? And how can they believe in the one of whom they have not heard? And how can they hear without someone preaching to them? And how can they preach unless they are sent?"

PHILEMON 6 – BE ACTIVE IN SHARING YOUR FAITH –

"I pray that you may be active in sharing your faith, so that you will have a full understanding of every good we have in Christ."

ACTS 22:15 – WE ARE HIS WITNESSES TO ALL MEN –

"You will be his witness to all men of what you have seen and heard."

ACTS 13:47 – BRING SALVATION TO THE ENDS OF THE EARTH –

"For this is what the Lord has commanded us: 'I have made you a light for the Gentiles, that you may bring salvation to the ends of the earth'."

II CORINTHIANS 4:1-6 – SPEAK PLAINLY THE TRUTH OF GOD TO THOSE WHO HAVE SEEN THE LIGHT OF GOD –

"Therefore, since through God's mercy we have this ministry, we do not lose heart. Rather, we have renounced secret and shameful ways; we do not use deception, nor do we distort the word of God. On the contrary, by setting forth the truth plainly, we commend ourselves to every man's conscience in the sight of God.

And even if our gospel is veiled, it is veiled to those who are perishing. The god of this age has blinded the minds of unbelievers, so that they cannot see the light of the gospel of the glory of Christ, who is the image of God.

"For we do not preach ourselves, but Jesus Christ as Lord, and ourselves as your servants for Jesus' sake. For God who said, 'Let light shine out of darkness', made His light shine in our hearts to give us the light of the knowledge of the glory of God in the face of Christ."

II CORINTHIANS 5:10 – OUR WORKS WILL BE REVEALED AT THE JUDGMENT SEAT OF CHRIST –

"For we must all appear before the judgment seat of Christ, that each one may receive what is due him for the things done while in the body, whether good or bad."

II CORINTHIANS 5:11-21 – WE TRY TO PERSUADE MEN OF THE TRUTH OF GOD. WE ARE COMMISSIONED TO BE CHRIST'S AMBASSADORS –

"Since, then, we know what it is to fear the Lord, we try to persuade men. What we are us plain to God, and I hope it is also plain to your conscience. We are not trying to commend ourselves to you again, but are giving you an opportunity to take pride in us, so that you can answer those who take pride in what is seen, rather than in what is in the heart."

"If we are out of our mind, it is for the sake of God. If we are in our right mind, it is for you. For Christ's love compels us, because we are convinced that one died for all, and therefore all died. And he died for us that those who live should no longer live for themselves but for him who died for them and was raised again."

"So, from now on we regard no one from a worldly point of view. Though we once regarded Christ in this way, we do so no longer. Therefore, if anyone is in Christ, he is a new creation; the old has gone; the new has come. All this is from God, who reconciled us to Himself through Christ and gave us the ministry of reconciliation, that God was reconciling the world to Himself in Christ, not counting men's sins against them. And he has committed to us the message of reconciliation."

"We are therefore Christ's ambassadors, as though God were making His appeal through us. We implore you on Christ's behalf: Be reconciled to God. God made him who had no sin to be sin for us, so that in him we might become the righteousness of God."

MARK 1:16, 17 – JESUS SAID, "I WILL MAKE YOU FISHERS OF MEN. QUESTION: ARE YOU FISHERS OF MEN? –

"As Jesus walked beside the Sea of Galilee, he saw Simon and his brother Andrew casting a net into the lake, for they were fishermen. 'Come, follow me', Jesus said, 'and I will make you fishers of men'."

THE PROMISE ABOUT SALVATION

ACTS 16:31 – "Believe in the Lord Jesus, and you will be saved – you and your household."

ROMANS 10:9 – "If you confess with your mouth, 'Jesus is Lord', and believe in your heart that God raised him from the dead, you will be saved."

ROMANS 10:13 – "For everyone who calls on the name of the Lord will be saved."

COLOSSIANS 1:13 – "For he has rescued us from the dominion of darkness and brought us into the kingdom of the Son He loves, in Whom we have redemption, the forgiveness of sin."

THE REWARDS OF ACCEPTING JESUS AS SAVIOR

JOHN 3:18 – "Whoever believes in Him is not condemned, but whoever does not believe stands condemned already because he has not believed in the name of God's one and only Son."

JOHN 3:36 – "Whoever believes in the Son has eternal life, but whoever rejects the Son will not see life, for God's wrath remains on him."

JOHN 6:40 – "Everyone who looks to the Son and believes in him, shall have eternal life, and I will raise him up at the last day."

HOW TO KNOW IF WE ARE CHRISTIANS:

I JOHN 2:3-6 – "We know that we have come to know him if we obey his commands. The man who says, 'I know him', but does not do what he commands, is a liar, and the truth is not in him. But if anyone obeys his word, God's love is truly made complete in him. This is how we know we are in him: Whoever claims to live in him must walk as Jesus did."

GOD HAS ASSIGNED EACH OF US TO OUR TASK.

I Cor. 3:5-9 – "What, after all, is Apollos? And what is Paul? Only servants through whom you came to believe – as the Lord has assign to each his task. I planted the seed, Apollos watered it, but God made it grow. So, neither he who plants nor he who waters is anything, but only God, who makes things grow. The man who plants and the man who waters have one pur- pose, and each will be rewarded according to his own labor. For we are God's fellow workers; you are God's field, God's building."

THE END TIMES REWARD OF OUR MINISTRY:

I Thess. 4:16-18 – "For the Lord himself will come down from heaven with a loud com- mand, with the voice of the archangel and with the trumpet call of God, and the dead in Christ will rise first. After that, we who are still alive and are left will be caught up with them in the clouds to meet the Lord in the air. And so we will be with the Lord forever. Therefore, encourage each other with these words."

ROMANS CHAPTERS 7 & 8

Romans chapter 7 is a very interesting and a challenging dialogue because it deals with our humanity and spirituality. Our carnal nature is to serve self. But, when God lives within us, our spiritual nature should be to serve God by serving others. There is a continual war within us to serve self or to serve God. The victory of that war is determined by which side we feed and yield to, and which side we choose to serve. This is a fact we must know. Jesus came to show us how to honor our Father by serving His people.

Satan is the god of deception, pain, and misery. With regard to deception, he can manipulate our thinking to justify our sin. He can cause our thinking to justify our self-serving desires. He can manipulate the scriptures to make us feel good about serving self. Probably, in my opinion, the biggest manipulation is that of apathy in the church by those who call themselves Christians. The church feels good about building bigger and bigger organizations and buildings while ignoring the poor and needy. Oh yes, the church may throw a token amount to the least of these, but its real passion is about the church organization instead of the welfare "of the least of these" as referred to in Matthew 25. We feel o.k. and comfortable watching the unsaved go to hell or the poor to go unattended to. WOW. The world is being given over to Satan and it is not the fault of the unsaved, but rather, those who have been called by Jesus. The Christians have the answers, so they must go out into the world.

In the first 12 chapters of Romans, Paul is explaining to the reformed Jews and converted Jews why the plan of salvation was offered to the Gentiles when the covenant of a personal relationship with God was given to the Jews through

His covenant with Abraham. That covenant is still in place. The Jews were the elect and still are the elect. But, because Jews rejected God through their disobedience, God opened up His plans to offer a personal relationship with Himself to the Gentiles. God did this to make the Jews jealous of the Gentiles, so that the Jews could come to Him. It did not work, because the Jews wanted to cling to the laws to defy their righteousness. This was a big issue that Paul had to address. He addressed this issue in the book of Romans.

Jesus came to bring a new covenant that changed the method of holy righteousness. Now the method of righteousness is through faith in Jesus and the grace of God through Jesus. The change in the method of acquiring holy righteousness is clearly expressed in Romans 1:17: "For in the gospel, a righteousness from God is revealed, a righteousness that is by faith from first to last, just as is written: 'The righteous will live by faith' ". The Jews felt salvation was exclusive to the Jews because of God's covenant with Abraham, so they clung to the law as a way of life and to achieve righteousness through the law. The Jews missed the message of Jesus and the new covenant.

Now, as to the covenant God made with Abraham about offering this covenant of a personal relationship with Him, it is still in place. What was given to Abraham is now offered to the Gentiles. If we Christians accept His son, Jesus, as a Godly blood offering to cancel the inherited sin of Adam (no matter who it is, Jew or Gentile), we will be grafted into the vine of Judaism and share in the root of the covenant with Abraham. We Christians call that covenant relationship with God the salvation experience. Consider Romans 11:11-14:

Again, I ask: Did they stumble so as to fall beyond recovery? Not at all. Rather, because of their transgression, salvation has come to the Gentiles to make Israel envious. But, if their transgression means riches to the world, and their loss means riches for the Gentiles, how much greater riches will their full-ness bring".

"I am talking to you Gentiles. In as much as I am the apostle to the Gentiles, I make much of my ministry in the hope that I may somehow arouse my own people to envy and save some of them. For if their rejection is the reconcili-ation of the world, what will their acceptance be but life from the dead? If the part of the dough offered as first fruits is holy, then the whole batch is holy; if the root is holy, so are the branches.

"If some of the branches have been broken off, and you, though a wild olive shoot, have been grafted in among the others and now share in the nourishing sap from the olive root, do not boast over those branches. If you do, consider this: You do not support the root, but the root supports you. You will say then, 'Branches were broken off so that I could be grafted'. But they were broken off because of unbelief, and you stand by faith. Do not be arrogant, but be afraid. For if God did not spare the natural branches, he will not spare you either."

"Consider therefore the kindness and sternness of God – sternness to those who fell, but kind-ness to you, provided that you continue in his kindness. Otherwise, you also will be cut off. And if they do not persist in unbelief, they will be grafted in, for God is able to graft them in again. After all, if you were cut out of an olive tree that is wild by nature, and contrary to nature were grafted into a cultivated olive tree, how much more readily will these, the natural branches, be grafted into their own olive tree!"

With regard to this grafting, consider Galatians 3:26-29: "You are all sons of God through faith in Christ Jesus. For all of you who were baptized into Christ have clothed yourselves with Christ. There is neither Jew or Greek, slave or free, male or female, for you are all one in Christ Jesus. If you belong to Christ, then you are Abraham's seed and heirs according to the promise".

IT IS CLEAR THAT GOD'S COVENANT WAS MADE WITH ABRAHAM. AND MAN'S ONLY WAY TO BE WITH GOD WAS THROUGH THAT COVENANT. JESUS CAME TO PROVIDE THE ONLY WAY TO BE GRAFTED INTO THAT COVENANT BY BEING GRAFTED INTO THE VINE OF THE FIRST CHOSEN OF JUDAISM."

Now, back to Romans chapter 7 – Since the Jews wanted to cling to the law as a method unto righteousness, Paul had to deal with specifics of how the law related and interacted with the new covenant. A personal relationship with God was not through the law, but was through faith in Jesus Christ and by God's grace. (I will discuss the law later.)

Now, with regard to the law and its controlling force over Paul and each of us – Note: the law was put in place to define the sin of the first covenant. THE PURPOSE OF THE LAW (very important) is stated in Romans 7:5, 6. If we miss this, we have missed everything.

Romans 7:5, 6: "For when we were controlled by the sinful nature, the sinful passions aroused by the law were at work in our bodies, so that we bore fruit for death.

But now, by dying to what once bound us, we have been released from the law so that we

SERVE in the new way of the spirit and not in the old way of the written code".

THE STRUGGLE

The struggle – Paul discusses the three elements of his struggle and our struggle with serving god by sanctifying our self through the new covenant of God using His standard of righteousness. There is a constant interaction between the three elements within us. These elements are the MIND, the BODY, and the SPIRIT.

MIND – Satan can play with the mind to deceive it, to desire, and do unholy things that are against God's standard of righteousness.

BODY – The carnal, feel good things of the body, can cause the mind to think sinful things that only serve the body.

SPIRIT – The spirit is that innate sense of right and wrong that is in us, that was given to us by God and illustrated through His son Jesus Christ.

> "For example, by law, a married woman is bound to her husband as long as he is alive, but if her husband dies, she is released from the law of marriage. So, then, if she marries another man while her husband is still alive, she is called an adulteress. But, if her husband dies, she is released from the law and is not an adulteress, even though she marries another man". – Romans 7:2,3

The word "law" is most often referred to as the law set into place in the book of Leviticus. The law of Leviticus is a requirement to be in fellowship with God. Obedience to the law was set as a standard of obedience and also a first covenant measure of obedience to righteousness. The Jews wanted to maintain those laws to separate themselves from the Gentiles. The laws, as they were written, were a function of <u>duty</u> and works. Jesus brought the new covenant of grace, faith, and a <u>desire</u> to love the Lord. The covenants went from <u>duty</u> to <u>desire</u>.

Now, back to Paul and his internal struggle of those three forces acting on him: His body is driven by carnal pleasure; his mind deals with Satan and his deception, and God's Holy Spirit within Paul is fighting to conquer Satan's deceptions with a holy relationship with God. It is like there is a raging war within him. I can identify with that raging war, because I also have that same war. Can you identify with the war? Well, Paul concedes that the dark side of that war has more power than he has. He is a slave to the evil side of those forces. Read Romans 7:21-25:

> "So I find this law at work. When I want to do good, evil is right there with me. For in my inner being, I delight in God's law, but I see another law at work in the members of my body, waging war against the law of my mind and making me a prisoner of the law of sin at work within my members. What a wretched man I am! Who will rescue me from this body of death? Thanks be to God – through Jesus Christ our Lord. So, then, I myself in my mind am a slave to God's law, but in the sinful nature, a slave to the law of sin".

Now, if Paul, as well as you and I, cannot compete with the evil side of our nature (By the way, the evil side is Satan), are we doomed to death and sin? NO, NO, NO. We have a POWER greater, <u>much greater</u>, than the power of Satan. Thanks to the power of Jesus, we can conquer the power of Satan. Read Romans 8:1-19:

"Therefore, there is now no condemnation for those who are in Christ Jesus, because through Christ Jesus, the law of the Spirit of life set me free from the law of sin and death. For what the law was powerless to do in that it was weakened by the sinful nature, God did by sending his own Son in the likeness of sinful man to be a sin offering. And so he condemned sin in sinful man in order that the righteous requirements of the law might be fully met in us, who do not live according to the sinful nature, but according to the Spirit".

"Those who live according to the sinful nature have their minds set on what that nature desires, but those who live in accordance with the spirit have their minds set on what the Spirit desires. The mind of sinful man is death, but the mind controlled by the Spirit is life and peace; the sinful mind is hostile to God. It does not submit to God's law, nor can it do so. Those controlled by the sinful nature cannot please God".

"You, however, are controlled not by the sinful nature but by the Spirit, if the Spirit of God lives in you. And if anyone doesn't have the Spirit of Christ, he does not belong to Christ. But if Christ is in you, your body is dead because of sin, yet your spirit is alive because of righteousness. And if the Spirit of him who raised Jesus from the dead is living in you, he who raised Christ from the dead will also give life to your mortal bodies through his spirit who lives in you".

"Therefore, brothers, we have an obligation –
but it is not to the sinful nature to live according
to it. For if you live according to the sinful
nature, you will die; but if by the Spirit you put
to death the misdeeds of the body, you will
live, because those who are led by the Spirit of
God are sons of God. For you did not receive a
spirit that makes you a slave again to fear, but
you received the Spirit of sonship. And by him,
we cry 'Abba Father'. The Spirit himself testifies
with our spirit that we are God's children. Now
if we are children, then we are heirs – heirs of
God and co-heirs with Christ, if indeed we share
in his sufferings in order that we may also share
in his glory."

"I consider that our present sufferings are not
worth comparing with the glory that will be
revealed in us. The creation waits in eager
expectation for the sons of God to be revealed."

Read these verses several times. These verses are our only
hope. Especially pay attention to chapter 8:1-4:

"Therefore, there is no condemnation for those
who are in Christ Jesus, because through Christ
Jesus, the law of the Spirit of life set me free
from the law of sin and death. For what the
law was powerless to do in that it was weakened by the sinful nature, God did by sending
his own son in the likeness of sinful man to
be a sin offering. And so he condemned sin in
sinful man in order that the righteous requirements of the law might be fully met in us who

do not live according to the sinful nature, but according to the Spirit."

The Law and the Derivation if its Origin - Watch the progression:

1. The sin of Adam: When Adam and Eve sinned, it angered God. He gave Adam and Eve dominion over everything in the Garden of Eden. Eve wanted more. She wanted dominion over God. This angered God, so He turned Satan loose to fight for their souls. He also removed them from the Garden of Eden. But, before they were removed, they asked for a covering of their nakedness and sin.

The scriptures do not say this, but I believe the first blood ever given was the blood of an innocent animal to provide a covering. That is why the first and original covenant between God and man was the covenant of blood and that covenant is still in place. Read Hebrews 9:16-22:

"In the case of a will, it is necessary to prove the death of the one who made it because a will is in force only when somebody has died; it never takes effect while the one who made it is living. This is why even the first covenant was not put into effect without blood. When Moses had proclaimed every commandment of the law to all the people, he took the blood of calves, together with water, scarlet wool and branches of hyssop and sprinkled the scroll and all the people."

"He said, 'This is the blood of the covenant which God has commanded you to keep. In the same way, he sprinkled with the blood both the tabernacle and everything used in its ceremonies.

In fact, the law requires that nearly everything
be cleansed with blood, and without the shedding of blood, there is no forgiveness".

Verse 22 –

"In fact, the law requires that nearly everything
be cleansed with blood and without the shedding of blood, there is no forgiveness."

Verse 22 clearly states that apart from the blood of the
covenant, there is no forgiveness, which became a law. Note:
An interesting thought – When Jesus said He came to fulfill
the law – was He referring to this original law of the blood of
the covenant?

2. God's invisible qualities of right and wrong. Read Romans
1:18-20:

"The wrath of god is being revealed from heaven
against all the godlessness and wickedness of
men who suppress the truth by their wickedness, since what may be known about God
is plain to them since God has made it plain
to them. For since the creation of the world,
God's invisible qualities – his eternal power and
divine nature – have been clearly seen, being
understood from what has been made, so that
men are without excuse."

NOTE: All of God's laws of his righteousness were put within
us at birth and we are without excuse.

3. The Ten commandments. The next set of laws was the Ten
Commandments. We should all know these commandments.

Man defied these commandments, so God put into place the Levitical laws.

NOTE: Jesus reformed the Ten Commandments. He did not change the Ten Commandments, he simplified them. NOTE: Matthew 22:35-40:

> "One of them, an expert in the law, tested Jesus with this question: 'Teacher, what is the greatest commandment in the Law?' Jesus replied, 'Love the Lord your God with all your heart and with all your soul and with all your mind. This is the first and greatest commandment. And the second is like it. "Love your neighbor as yourself.' All the Law and the prophets hang on these two commandments."

NOTE: Then, later, Jesus added a new commandment: John 13:34-35:

> "A new commandment I give you: Love one another. As I have loved you, so you must love one another. By this all men will know that you are my disciples, if you love one another."

4. <u>The Levitical Laws</u>. These laws were work based and they were labor intense. These laws were almost impossible to keep and for a purpose. These laws were designed to show man that by his works, apart from God, he could never win the complete approval of God. These laws set the stage for the last and final method of approval by God.

5. <u>God's grace and our faith</u>. God brought forth a completely new Disposition – the disposition of God's grace and

faith in Jesus Christ. God's approval of us is through the original blood covenant where Jesus gave His blood for the redemption of our sin. Our redemption of sin and our way into heaven is through God's grace and to believe Jesus is the Son of God, and his son gave his blood to pay for our sin.

THE BOND BETWEEN GOD AND MAN AS TO THE BOND BETWEEN HUSBAND AND WIFE

A special note: Paul begins his discussion of the bond that is made between man and God with an illustration of the first covenant bond between a husband and his wife. It was a covenant that was never to be broken or breached. The details of that covenant of marriage were very precise, as is the details of the covenant between man and God. Notice chapter 7:2,3:

> "For example, by law, a married woman is bound to her husband as long as he is alive, but if her husband dies, then she is released from the law of marriage. So then, if she marries another man while her husband is still alive, she is called an adulteress. But, if her husband dies, she is released from that law and is not an adulteress even though she marries another man."

Notice: God gave no deviation or compromise or exception. Saved or not saved, a woman should not remarry while her husband is still alive. I do not understand this, but it does not matter if I understand it or agree or disagree. God commanded it, not I. I do know this: We all have sinned and we are still sinners. As Paul has stated, it is through our sin that we are made unworthy which causes us to <u>need</u> the saving Grace of Jesus Christ.

This marriage covenant that Paul was referring to was a law of the <u>first</u> covenant. Is that covenant still in effect? You decide.

This appears to be an amendment to that first covenant. That amendment appears as new rules or laws of the new covenant. Consider I Corinthians 7:1-40.

I Corinthians 7:1-14: "Now for the matters you wrote about, it is good for a man not to marry. But since there is so much immorality, each man should have his own wife, and each woman should have her own husband. The husband should fulfill his marital duty to his wife, and likewise, the wife to her husband. The wife's body does not belong to her alone, but also to her husband. In the same way, the husband's body does not belong to him alone, but also to his wife. Do not deprive each other except by mutual consent and for a time, so that you may devote yourselves to prayer. Then come together again so that Satan will not tempt you because of your lack of self control. I say this as a concession, not as a command. I wish that all men were as I am. But each man has his own gift from God; one has this gift, another has that".

"Now to the unmarried and the widows, I say it is good for them to stay unmarried as I am. But if they cannot control themselves, they should marry, for it is better to marry than to burn with passion".

"To the married, I give this command (not I, but the Lord). A wife must not separate from her husband. But, if she does, she must remain unmarried or else be reconciled to her husband. And a husband must not divorce his wife".

> "To the rest, I say this (I and not the Lord). If any brother has a wife who is not a believer and she is willing to live with him, he must not divorce her. And if a woman has a husband who is not a believer and he is willing to live with her, she must not divorce him. For the unbelieving husband has been sanctified through his wife, and the unbelieving wife has been sanctified through her believing husband. Otherwise, your children would be unclean, but as it is, they are holy".

What you have read as God's rules as it pertains to un married and married relationships. The rules (laws) are very clear.

Another rule or law of the new covenant is Matthew 5:27-32 which deals with adultery and divorce:

> "You have heard it said, 'Do not commit adultery'. But I tell you that anyone who looks at a woman lustfully has already committed adultery with her in his heart. If your right eye causes you to sin, gouge it out and throw it away. It is better for you to lose one part of your body than for your whole body to be thrown into hell. And if your right hand causes you to sin, cut it off and throw it away. It is better for you to lose one part of your body than for your whole body to go into hell".

> "It has been said that 'Anyone who divorces his wife must give her a certificate of divorce'. But I tell you that anyone who divorces his wife, except for marital unfaithfulness, causes her to commit adultery, and anyone who marries a woman so divorced commits adultery".

WOW. God is laying out some very tough stuff. He is giving references of being thrown into hell and setting the standards and rules of divorce. God must consider this covenant between a man and a woman as a sacred covenant, comparable to His covenant between Himself and man. This is serious business!

Interesting note: Paul's thorn in his flesh. There has always been a lot of speculation of what that thorn was. I think the thorn may be related to the raging war of good and evil that was within him, as he discussed in Romans Chapter 7. Read II Corinthians 12:7-10:

> "To keep me from becoming conceited because of these surpassing revelations, there was given me a thorn in my flesh, a messenger of Satan, to torment me. Three times I pleaded with the Lord to take it away from me. But he said to me, 'My grace is sufficient for you, for my power is made perfect in weakness'. Therefore, I will boast all the more gladly about my weaknesses, so that Christ's power may rest on me. That is why, for Christ's sake, I delight in weaknesses, in insults, in hardships, in persecutions, in difficulties. For when I am weak, then I am strong".

Note: The thorn was given to him by a messenger of Satan to torture him. That is an interesting thought.

Hopefully, what I have written will give you something to consider.

Romans 8:28

"And we know that all things work together for good to those who love the Lord"

I have heard this phrase used in dozens of ways for dozens of purposes. It has been used to rationalize weakness and failure. It has been used to justify and glorify self worth. It needs to be used to gratify a beautiful, trusting relationship with the Lord.

The intent of the phrase does not stop where most people let it stop. The scripture goes on as follows - And we know that all things work together for good to those who love God, to those who are the called according to His purpose" (vs. 28). "For whom He foreknew, He also predestined to be conformed to the image of His Son that He might be the firstborn among many brethren" (vs. 29). Moreover whom He predestined, these He also called, these He also justified and whom He justified, these He also glorified" (vs. 30).

Notice: The trailing part of verse 28 qualified who this Scripture applies to by saying, "who have been called according to His purpose." Question: WHO HAS BEEN CALLED according to His purpose? Verses 29 and 30 clarify that. Verse 29: "For whom He foreknew, He also predestined to be conformed to the image of His Son that He might be the firstborn among many brethren." The key that reveals the persons, those who have been called to His purpose, are those "who were predestined to be conformed to the likeness of His Son." That commitment means to search for God's standards of righteousness and live by those standards by God's help. Verse 30 goes on to say "Those He called, He also justified; those He justified, He also glorified." Notice verse 29. Question: Are you conformed to a likeness of His Son? If you are, then this verse applies to you. If you are justified through faith, trust and works that glorify the Lord, your life should reveal those attributes.

Now, back to verse 28. "In all things God works for those good to those WHO LOVE HIM." Question: The big question is "who loves Him". This question does not have an easy answer. To find the answer, go back to Romans Chapter 7. The answer starts there. Paul talks about the sin nature we have within us that was born within us at birth because of the sin of Adam. We were born with a law of sin which leads to a sinful nature and to a spiritual death that wins us a place in Hell at our physical death. Paul also talks about the law of righteousness. By the grace of God, we are shown the law of righteousness and grace. Paul says the law of righteousness reveals the law of sin. Because of these two laws struggling within us, we have to choose which law we intend to follow: the law of sin or the law of righteousness. The law of sin leads to hell and righteousness leads to heaven.

Paul himself (who wrote 2/3 of the New Testament) had a struggle with these two laws. It is as though there are two forces fighting for your soul. Paul testified to this struggle as stated in Romans 7:15-20:

> (15.) "I do not understand what I do. For what I want to do, I do not do, but what I hate, I do. (16.) And if I do what I do not want to do, I agree the law is good.

> (17.) As it is, it is no longer I who do it, but it is sin living in me. (18.) I know that nothing good lives in me, that is, in my sinful nature. For I have the desire to do what is good, but I cannot carry it out.

> (19.) For what I do is not the good I want to do; no, the evil I do not want to do – this I keep on doing. (20.) Now if I do what I do not want to do, it is no longer I who do it, but it is sin living in me that does it. "O wretched man that I am! Who will deliver me from this body of death? I thank God - through Jesus Christ our Lord! So, then, with the mind I myself serve the law of God, but with the flesh, the law of sin."

Paul said "thanks be to God – through Jesus Christ our Lord." That is the only way to fight and win over sin. WOW!

Spiritual Nature – When you realize what Jesus did on the cross to conquer sin, you must also realize that you must fight the battle of your sinful nature and live for God's plan of righteousness. This fight is a choice you must make. It is a choice. Read Romans 8:5-11:

> (5.) "For those who live according to the flesh set their minds on the things of the flesh, but those who live according to the Spirit, the things of the Spirit.

> (6.) "For to be carnally minded is death, but to be spiritually minded is life and peace.

> (7.) "Because the carnal mind is enmity against God; for it is not subject to the law of God, nor indeed can be.

> (8.) "So then, those who are in the flesh cannot please God.

> (9.) "But you are not in the flesh but in the Spirit, if indeed the Spirit of God dwells in you. **Now if anyone does not have the Spirit of Christ, he is not His.**

> (10.) And if Christ is in you, the body is dead because of sin, but the Spirit is life because of righteousness.

> (11.) "But if the Spirit of Him who raised Jesus from the dead who dwells in you, He who raised Christ from the dead dwells in you. He who raised Christ from the dead will also give

life to your mortal bodies through His Spirit
who dwells in you."

Paul is very clear in these Scriptures about who has a sinful
or spiritual nature. Also, about how a person acquires and nur-
tures a sinful or spiritual nature. Paul is also very clear about
who does not belong go God. Verse 9 – "But you are not in
the flesh but in the Spirit, if indeed the Spirit of God dwells in
you. **Now if anyone does not have the Spirit of Christ, he is
not His.** It is also logical that if someone does not belong to
God, he cannot love Him.

Now back to Romans 8:28 "In all things God works for the
good of those who love Him". The big question – **Who is it that
really loves Him?** It seems clear to me that if a person really
loves God through Jesus, that person would seek to be conformed to the likeness of His Son and also to be justified by
faith through the blood of Jesus which was given at the event
of the cross. Next, I would go on to say if you really knew the
price of your salvation, you would be compelled to sanctification and to do works in order to glorify the Lord.

Now back to Romans 8:28. "In all things God works for
the GOOD of those who LOVE HIM. Question: God works for
the GOOD of those who love him. The question is what does
GOOD mean? Most peoples' perception of GOOD is a victory or
defeat of a preconceived outcome. Most of the time the preconceived outcome is short term and is in terms that person
can understand without much consideration of what God considers good and necessary. The true meaning of what God considers good may involve short term victories, but may also
involve distressful and the agonizing circumstances of our life
process that you may never understand. What may be good to
some may also cause others distress and pain. To really understand what is truly GOOD, we must trust that GOD is sovereign
and will use all things for our long term good and to his glory,
even if we don't understand the circumstances of God's plan.

This scripture, "In all things, God works for the good of those who love him." – It is used so frequently out of context, and therefore, has no spiritual or tangible value to our lives when it is used out of the context of its true meaning.

Question: Who does this Scripture apply to? Read for yourself, study and analyze this report and come to your own conclusion. It has been my observation that Romans 8:28 is very specific to only a few.

SATAN AND HELL

Satan is a real being and hell is a real place. Some denominations and theologians denounce or minimize the power of Satan and the place of hell. Wow! I would not want to be in their place at judgment day. Some preachers and teachers do not approach the subject of Satan or hell. Why? Jesus referred to hell more than any other subject. Because preachers and teachers do not discuss the subject of Satan or hell, their congregations do not fear Satan or hell, which could cause the congregation to feel comfortable in their own sin, which could lead to eternity in hell. If people do not understand the deceptions of Satan or fear the consequences of hell, then there may not be a need for repentance of sin. Without repentance of sin, a person cannot achieve righteousness. Without God's righteousness, heaven may not be attainable.

Outlined below is a very brief discussion of Satan and hell. Hopefully, this discussion will inspire you to study these topics for your own personal understanding.

SATAN

Satan, or the devil as we refer to, actually was first named Lucifer. Lucifer was the name given to the angel that God created to be perfect when he lived in heaven. Lucifer sinned against God. After Lucifer sinned against God, he was thrown out of heaven and then became known as Satan, or the Devil. In the beginning, Lucifer was created by God as a perfect angel. Lucifer lost favor with God when he tried to usurp the authority of God. In the beginning, God created many angels. Lucifer was the perfect angel. When God threw Lucifer out of heaven, 30% of the angels went with him. He was then renamed Satan, or the Devil, and his nature became a beast of deception, pain and hate. Those angels that went with Satan became the enemies of God just as Satan did. These angels became demons and workers for Satan's purpose. Satan's power and authority were controlled and confined until Adam committed the great sin of eating of the forbidden fruit. When Adam ate of the forbidden fruit, Satan and his angels were released to fight for the souls of men (and women). When Lucifer was thrown out of heaven, he was angry and resented God. He wanted to hurt God, so he went out to steal God's most treasured and valued possessions, man and woman. It started at the sin of Adam and exists to this day. Satan wants to steal the souls of man and God wants to save the souls of man. Because God is a fair and loving God, He gave man and woman a choice to choose which God they wanted to serve. The choice is ours. That choice sounds simple, but it is not that simple. Because of the sin of Adam and Eve's selfishness, all of their descendants, which include you and me, were born with a desire to serve self, even to the detriment of others. Serving self became the basis of all sin.

Note: There is a divine war going on between heavenly powers - the power of God's righteousness of love, mercy, grace, giving and forgiving AND Satan's power of deception to serve self. Satan's power to deceive man has been enhanced by man's inherited nature from Adam to serve self.

Question: What is bad about serving self, even to the extent of hurting others? At first glance, serving self seems o.k., but over the long run, it leads to pain and sorrow and enmity among men, which is not good. Well, God had a plan for his creation. That plan was for man to be happy, loved, fulfilled, and to live in total harmony. The only way that can be accomplished is if we give to others – not take from others. God wants us to love one another and to show mercy, to give and to forgive. If we can do that, man can live in total harmony and have joy and be happy. If that were accomplished where man lived in total harmony, that would defeat Satan's purpose of revenge against God by destroying man. Satan's goals are to hurt, torture and destroy man. And in doing that, he steals God's greatest love and possession. That would serve as his revenge against God.

Question: What is Satan's greatest tool to capture the souls of man? Deception! The whole area of sin started when he was able to deceive Eve into eating of the forbidden fruit. Deception is still his most valuable tool. Romans Chapter 1 says that Satan will deceive a person to the point that man will not be able to distinguish good from bad. What is bad will seem to be good. What is good will seem to be bad. The next deception – man will be attracted to man and women will be attracted to women. Then, because man has bought into the deception, God will allow his mind to be turned into a reprobate mind. WOW! Deception will steal the lives of man on earth and send them into eternal torment. Remember, Satan wants your body and soul, so he can torture you and in doing so – hurt God.

Note: Satan was the greatest angel and acquired a great power of deception. Based on your own strength, he will conquer you. Satan is mighty, strong and relentless. Question: What is our greater power to conquer Satan, and what is our hope? Paul addressed this issue in Romans 7:24,25 and Romans 8:1-11

> Romans 7:24,25: "What a wretched man I am! Who will rescue me from this body of

death? Thanks be to God – through Jesus Christ our Lord!"

Romans 8:1-11:"Therefore, there is now no condemnation for those who are in Christ Jesus, because through Christ Jesus, the law of the Spirit of life set me free from the law of sin and death. For what the law was powerless to do in that it was weakened by the sinful nature, God did by sending His own Son in the likeness of sinful man to be a sin offering. And he condemned sin in sinful man, in order that the righteous requirements of the law might be fully met in us, who do not live according to the sinful nature, but according to the Spirit."

"Those who live according to the sinful nature have their minds set on what that nature desires, but those who live in accordance with the Spirit have their minds set on what the Spirit desires. The mind of the sinful man is death, but the mind controlled by the Spirit is life and peace; the sinful mind is hostile to God. It does not submit to God's law nor can it do so. Those controlled by the sinful nature cannot please God.

"You, however, are controlled not by the sinful nature, but by the Spirit, if the Spirit of God lives in you. And if anyone does not have the Spirit of Christ, he does not belong to Christ. But, if Christ is in you, your body is dead because of sin, yet your spirit is alive because of righteousness. And if the Spirit of him who raised Jesus from the dead is living in you, he who raised Christ

from the dead will also give life to your mortal
bodies through his Spirit who lives in you."

WOW! We can have power over Satan if we have the Spirit
living within us. Question: How can we have the Spirit of God
within us? Answer: Only if we give our life to Jesus – the Son of
God – and being born again, repenting of our sins and, most of
all, believing that Jesus died and gave His blood to pay for our
sins. If we do that and believe in our hearts, we will be saved
from hell. At that time, the Spirit of God will enter in and live
within you. The Spirit living within you will be your protector
and source of strength to recognize sin and to conquer sin. The
Spirit living within you is God living within you.

HELL

Hell – a real physical place, not a state of mind, a real place
known as the unseen underworld. It is a real place where the
body cannot and will not die, even though there is extreme
torture. The torture is described as pain that causes the teeth
to gnash and a relentless fire and heat and a place where
worms eternally eat the flesh. Dante, in The Divine Comedy,
describes his vision of a place in hell as – people running in an
eternal circle where the fire and heat is unbearable. As they
are running in this eternal circle, they are being stung by bees
and hornets. The people would tear off the bees and hornets
only to be replaced by more bees and hornets. As they tore off
the bees and hornets, they threw them to the floor where they
were eaten by maggots on the floor. The screams of pain and
agony were almost unbearable. Remember: This is an eternity
of torment.

Jesus spoke clearly about hell. While Jesus was clear about
hell and the consequences of hell, many theologians try to
minimize hell and its consequences. Jesus preached about hell
as much or more than any other subject. The New Testament

gives over 60 references to hell, and the word "hell" appears 23 times. The word "hell" appears 31 times in the Old Testament. Why is understanding the place of hell so important? Jesus knows about the place of hell. He knows the tortures of hell. Jesus also knows his Father God is a sinless God and lives in a place where sin cannot exist. In the beginning, God and Adam and Eve were sinless and lived in a sinless place called Eden. When Adam sinned, he became dirty, so God threw him out of his presence on earth. At some point, God made a provision for man to cleanse himself of sin so that man could once again be in the presence of God. That provision was the blood of a perfect being. Once that sin debt of blood was paid by the blood of a perfect being, then man could once again stand in the presence of God. If that sin debt was not paid, man would go into eternal torment – a place called hell. Now, for more than a thousand years, man failed to meet the blood standard set by God, so Jesus came to earth to give the blood (His blood) for forgiveness of the sins of man, so that man would not have to go to hell, but, rather, stand in the presence of our holy God. That is the reason we need to know that hell is real. Jesus gave His life and blood so we would not have to go to hell, but, rather, go to heaven.

Listed below are some of many scriptures you can study to know more about hell:

> Luke 16:22-24: "The time came when the beggar died and the angels carried him to Abraham's side. The rich man also died and was buried. In hell, where he was in torment, he looked up and saw Abraham far away, with Lazarus by his side. So he called to him, "Father Abraham, have pity on me and send Lazarus to dip the tip of his finder in water and cool my tongue, because I am in agony in this fire."

Matthew 5:29,30: "If you right eye causes you to sin, gouge it out and throw it away. It is better for you to lose one part of your body than for your whole body to be thrown into hell. And if your right hand causes you to sin, cut it off and throw it away. It is better for you to lose one part of your body than for your whole body to go into hell."

Matthew 7:15-20: "Watch out for false prophets. They come to you in sheep's clothing, but inwardly they are ferocious wolves. By their fruit you will recognize them. Do people pick grapes from thorn bushes, or figs from thistles? Likewise, every good tree bears good fruit, but a bad tree bears bad fruit. A good tree cannot bear bad fruit, and a bad tree cannot bear good fruit. Every tree that does not bear good fruit is cut down and thrown into the fire. Thus, by their fruit, you will recognize them."

Luke 12:4,5:"I tell you, my friends, do not be afraid of those who kill the body and after than can do no more. But I will show you whom you should fear: Fear him who, after the killing of the body, has power to throw you into hell. Yes, I tell you, fear him."

Rev. 20:11-15: Then I saw a great white throne and him who was seated on it. Earth and sky fled from his presence, and there was no place for them. And I saw the dead, great and small, standing before the throne, and books were opened. Another book was opened, which is the book of life. The dead were judged according to what they had done as recorded in the books. The sea gave up the dead that were in it, and death and Hades gave up the dead that were in them, and each person was judged according to what he had done. Then death and Hades were thrown into the lake of fire. The lake of fire is the second death. If anyone's name was not found written in the book of life, he was thrown into the lake of fire."

These are only a few scriptures that refer to hell. Hell is not a good place. Question: Do you believe heaven exists? Do you believe hell exists? If you really, really, really believe there is a heaven and a hell, how could you ever take a chance of going to hell when it is sure you can go to heaven. God provided a way into heaven. Call me at 662-844-5307 if you want to know more.

CONCLUSION

Now you know. It is not heaven <u>and</u> hell. It is heaven <u>or</u> hell. Satan is the great deceiver and has a horrible plan for your life. God is the source of all truth and has a wonderful plan for your life. To serve Satan is to serve self. To serve God is to serve others. God sent His Son as a servant to show us how to serve others.

SUFFERING – WHY?

Maybe your suffering is for the sake of God. You know Joseph's story of suffering for the sake of God's purpose. It seems as though God accomplishes great life-altering events through the suffering of His chosen people. Jesus is the prime example. He suffered for our sin. With that said, I am reminded of an event that probably caused the greatest growth in the spreading of God's Word, and it involved suffering. It was the event of Stephen's death by stoning (Acts 7 and 8). When Stephen reminded the Jews of their sin and hypocrisy, they stoned him at the gate of Jerusalem. The Pharisees did not want to be reminded of their sin and hypocrisy, so they stoned Stephen to death. This was a significant event, and what made it more significant was that Paul was there and gave approval for the stoning death of Stephen. The suffering and death of Stephen caused the church at Jerusalem to scatter. When the church members scattered, they formed many other churches. When they scattered, the cause of Jesus Christ grew greatly. After Stephen's death, Paul was on his way to Damascus. Jesus confronted Paul on that road. Jesus renamed Saul to the name of Paul. The rest of that event is well known. God worked through Paul to write two-thirds of the New Testament. Paul was also tortured and suffered greatly for the cause of Jesus. Paul began to rejoice in his suffering for the cause of Jesus Christ.

Here is the point: If Stephen had not suffered and died for the sake of righteousness, where would we be today? What Stephen did through suffering set the course for the future of all mankind. Do you know that your suffering might have a great purpose for the sake of all mankind and for the sake of God's glory? What a privilege that would be to suffer for the sake of God. Give your suffering to God and see what happens.

THE ESSENCE OF THE BIBLE DEPICTED IN ONE BIBLE VERSE – JOHN 3:16

"For God so loved the world that He gave His one and Only Son, that whoever believes in Him shall not perish, but have eternal life."

Some time ago, I attended an event where Dr. David Jeremiah spoke on God's love. He made a very profound statement that essentially was this: The whole bible can be summed up in the verse John 3:16. That was a huge statement, so I decided to analyze that verse, John 3:16, to see if I could draw the same conclusion. Some of this analysis includes his thoughts. So, here we go.

"For God" – the first two words introduce who is making the statement that follows. That introduction would prompt the question – who is God and what authority does He have to make this statement? The answer is best defined in the first four words of the bible, Genesis 1:1 – "In the beginning God". That statement reveals that God existed before the beginning – He <u>was</u> the beginning. The verses that follow describe His authority when He created the world and had the power to speak all things into existence. He had the power to turn dust into flesh and to create a spirit that co-existed with the flesh. The spirit did not exist prior to that creation and had no tangible matter. He did this through Adam. The answer to Who is God and what authority does He have? - He is the author and finisher of all things. Nothing exists without His sovereign permission. This God of all authority is about to make the most profound declaration of all time.

"So" – This is an interesting word in its context. In its context, it describes how much God loves you. The word "so" has no dimension or no limit. God loves you beyond any known measure. He loves you "so" much.

"Loved" – This word is used as a verb. A verb denotes some form of action. The words that follow the word "loved" describe His actions for using the word "loved". Read and try to comprehend the depth of the words that follow.

"The World" – God defines the scope of His love. Notice He did <u>not</u> say the color of people, the class of people, people in any one country, etc. He said, "the world". When I am in the mission field in all of the different countries, I observe people praying and I realize they are all praying to the same God. These people are part of "the world". Some people in the world are praying for a clean glass of water, while others are praying for a higher comfort level. These are all God's people in "the world".

"That He gave" – to give is a voluntary action. God showed the greatest act of MERCY on humanity when He "gave" His Son to be crucified, which paid the penalty we would have had to pay for our sins. Yes, He "gave" His Son for our sin. God, Himself, crushed Him and caused Him to suffer on the cross. Read this quote from God's Word: "Yet it was the Lord's will to crush him and cause him to suffer, and though the Lord makes his life a guilt offering, he will see his offspring and prolong his days, and the will of the Lord will prosper in his hand". (Isaiah 53:10) God was faced with a decision: sacrifice His son for His people or sacrifice the people for His Son. He made that huge decision and "gave His son to be sacrificed. The price for redemption of sin was the blood of Jesus. God "gave" His son. Question: Does that describe how much God loves you?

"His One and Only Son" – Jesus was God, but He was also "His one and only son". God did not have another friend or companion. Jesus was His only Son and he and the Holy Spirit were his only companions. If He lost Jesus, He lost His only Son. If He lost Jesus, what was the purpose of creation? God made a choice to sacrifice His only son to pay the sin debt of your and my sins. He did that because He loves you and all of His creation that much. WOW! Do you really, really, really, realize that? If you truly did realize the cost of your salvation, you would be praising and thanking Him and would want to live to serve Him each and every moment of the day.

"That Whoever" – These words have no dimension and have no exclusiveness. Notice, it does not limit His love to any particular denomination, color, creed, nation, social status, wealth class or anything. He said "that <u>whoever</u>". Does "whoever" include the worst of sinners and the most righteous? Yes, it does. Now, the next words qualify "whoever" – I am glad that includes me and you.

"Believes in Him" – The word "believe" is a function of faith. The scriptures are filled with the messages of belief and faith. The opposite of belief and faith is to <u>know</u>. I do not know why God does what He does. All I know is that He does what He does. If He wants us to believe and have faith, that is up to Him. Actually, there will be a point in our life when we will no longer believe, but we will actually know. When we die and stand at judgment, we'll KNOW. "Whoever" – I am glad that includes me and you.

"Shall Not Perish" – The word "perish" means to be destroyed, or not to exist. The words "not perish" in this text means to <u>not</u> be separated from God. When our flesh dies, our soul continues to exist. If our soul perishes, it goes to hell for eternity. If our soul does <u>not</u> perish, it exists in eternal heaven which is in the presence of God. Oh, what a time of Glory!

"But Have Eternal Life" – Question: Can we even begin to understand eternity? Eternity is beyond our limit of understanding. To be in hell for eternity – Can you imagine that? To be in heaven for eternity – Can you imagine that! God is speaking of "eternal life". Question: What does eternal life mean? Our soul never dies. Our flesh was made of dust and will return to dust. Our soul will exist for eternity. The most important question for each of us is "Will our soul perish in hell or exist in heaven"?

Now, let's go back to the original postulate. Can the bible be summed up in one verse – John 3:16? My answer is "yes", in many ways. That verse describes "God's love" for us from the beginning, "God" to the end, "Eternal Life" and everything in between.

I would like to leave you with one question: Do you really appreciate the cost and value of your salvation? God <u>gave</u> His only son just for you. Your appreciation of that cost is shown by your love for Him and the way you serve Him. Is your appreciation shown by a church experience, or a religious experience, or a relationship experience?

THE GOSPEL AT A GLANCE

<u>In The Beginning</u> - All of creation is justified by the first four words in the Bible, "In the beginning God".

Genesis1:1 – God created the heavens and the earth.

Genesis 1:27 – God created man in His own image.

Genesis 1:28 – God told man to subdue the earth and gave him dominion.

<u>God Gave Heaven to Man, but Man Disobeyed and Sinned</u>.

Genesis 2:17 – "You must not eat from the tree of knowledge. If you do, surely you will die.

Genesis 23:6 – When the woman saw that the fruit of the tree was good for food and pleasing to the eye, and also she desired to gain wisdom, she ate it. She gave it to Adam, and he ate of it.

<u>The Penalty of Sin</u>

Genesis 3:17 – Because of their disobedience, God cursed their life, and all who followed with the pain and misery of survival.

Romans 6:23 – The wages of sin is death.

Hebrews 9:27 – Men die once and then comes the judgment.

<u>The Fact of Sin</u>

Romans 3:23 – All have sinned.

Romans 3:10 – There are none who are righteous.

I John 1:8 – If we say we have no sin, we have deceived ourselves.

<u>How Does Man Get Back to God?</u>

Titus 3:5 – Deeds? – He saves us not on the basis of deed.

Romans 3:20 – Works? – By works of law no flesh will be justified.

Proverbs 14:12 – Knowledge? – A way that seems right to man lead to death.

Does God Still Love Man?

John 3:16 – For God so loved the world that He gave His only Son to die on the cross for our sin.

I John 4:16 – God is love.

Luke 19:10 – The Son of Man came to seek and to save.

Galatians 1:4 – He gave Himself for our sin, that He would deliver us from our sin.

God Provided Jesus to Reunite Man Unto Himself.

Romans 5:18,19 – God demonstrated His love for us even though we were Sinners. Jesus died for our sin.

John 14:6 – Jesus said, "I am the way, the truth and the life".

Ephesians 1:7 – Through Jesus we have redemption of our sin through the blood of Jesus.

Acts 4:12 – Jesus is the only way unto salvation.

To Be Reunited With God, Man Must Make a Choice.

Acts 16:31 – Believe in the Lord Jesus – you shall be saved.

Romans 10:9 – Confess Jesus as Lord; believe in your heart and you shall be saved.

Acts 17:30 – God desires that all should repent.

Acts 4:12 – Salvation is found in no one else, for there is no other name under heaven given to man by which we might be saved.

If You Have Made The Right Choice – You Are Reconciled (Saved).

II Corinthians 5:17 – Therefore, if any man is in Christ, he is a new creation.

II Corinthians 5:19 – We are reconciled to God through Jesus, the Christ.

John 3:18 – He who believes in Him shall not be judged.

Romans 8:1 – No condemnation for those who are in Christ Jesus

Philippians 3:20 – Jesus provides for our citizenship in heaven.

The Great Commandment of Jesus to the Reconciled (Saved)
> Matthew 22:37-40 – Jesus said, "Love the Lord your
> God with all your Heart and with all your soul and with
> all your mind. This is the first and greatest command-
> ment. And the second like it: Love your neighbor as
> yourself".

The Great commission of God for the Reconciled (Saved)
> II Corinthians 3:6 – He has made us competent as min-
> isters of the New Covenant.
> Mark 1:17 – "Come follow me and I will make you
> fishers of men".
> John 17:17, 18 – "Sanctify them (the reconciled) by the
> truth. Your Word is truth. As You have sent me into the
> world, I have sent them into the world". The reason is
> that the reconciled are now His ambassadors.
> Matthew 28:19,20 – "Therefore, go and make disciples
> of all nations, baptizing them in the name of the Father
> and the Son and the Holy Spirit, teaching them to obey
> everything I have commanded you. And surely I am
> with you always, to the very end of the age".

Note: Some references are from an article of New Creation
Ministries.

THE REASON FOR TRUTH

The truth of God's creation is not a concern under my control. I am simply subject to that truth. What matters to me is
the pursuit of that truth. In the text of theology, what is true
is always true and what is false is always false. Truth cannot
change. Prior to the coming of Jesus, the truth of all creation
was given by God to certain men who were responsible for
disseminating that truth. They were most commonly referred
to as prophets. The Scriptures tell us in Hebrews that Jesus
came to fulfill the law and to begin a new dispensation and

reveal the last and complete truth to be given to man. When He came, we were released from all the Leviticus laws, rituals, sacrifices and services of the previous dispensation. We were given a new covenant (agreement between God and His people). Under the old covenant (agreement between God and His people), man, in general, could not look upon God or even be in the presence of God. God chose only a few to intercede on man's behalf and even then only at specified times. Jesus came to bring the new covenant whereby all men at any time can go directly to God through Him. The Bible says there is only one mediator now between God and man – Jesus (I Timothy 2:5). The priesthood is no longer needed or wanted (Hebrews 9:18-19). Another person, such as a priest or pastor, acting as a mediator is not only not needed any longer, but is actually not wanted in light of the dispensation to come. The Scripture says at the death of Jesus, the veil between man and the presence of God in the Holy of Holies (which only a priest could enter and only once a year), was ripped from top to bottom. This is all very important because now Jesus is the ONLY mediator between God and man. NOW JESUS AND HIS TRUTH (the Scriptures) will be the source of all truth.

In the last dispensation (the next dispensation to come), man and/or an organization will be part of the great deception. The great deception will ultimately try to reenact the previous dispensation that, among other things, separated man from God through the priesthood or prophets. That is what Jesus came and died to release us from. Basically, the great deception will try to once again elevate man or an entity, such as a church, as God. If that can be done then man can choose to live by the standard he devises. Time and again we are rebuked by Scripture to test all things to the new covenant. We are to test all human teachers, and yes, even the clergy. Any lion can wear the cloak of a sheep and for awhile appear to be a sheep. Therefore, truth and the basis of truth are very important. Jesus spoke in John 8:32 that the truth will set you free. This quote is misused by much of the Christian community as well as the secular community. Study the text of this verse, and you will see its correct meaning. The truth that the secular world has to offer does not set you free, but rather, makes you captive to it and you are enslaved by it. On the other hand, the truth of the Holy Father through Jesus Christ, who brought the indwelling of the Holy Spirit, does not enslave you, but rather, really sets you free. Why do I seek truth? Because it sets me free and I want to be free!

My final resolve is this: If Jesus is <u>not</u> who He said he was, then I do not have time for Him. If He <u>is</u> who He said He was, I <u>cannot</u> live apart from Him.

One of my favorite verses in the Old Testament is Proverbs 2:1-6:

> "My son, if you receive my words and treasure up my command within you, so that you incline your ear to wisdom and apply your heart to understanding; yes, if you cry out for discernment, and lift up your voice for understanding, if you seek her as silver, and search for her as gold, then you will understand the fear of the Lord and find the knowledge of God. For the Lord gives wisdom; From His mouth come knowledge and understanding.

THE SERMON ON THE MOUNT

Matthew 5 is often called "the Sermon on the Mount". Jesus spent a great deal of time detailing those things for which we are "blessed". The Greek word used for "blessed" is *makarios*, which means "supremely fortunate", "well-off". Consider the list below which Jesus included in blessings. It is not what most people would consider "well-off" or "supremely fortunate" in having. In fact, most are things we try hard to avoid.

JESUS SAID: "BLESSED ARE:
THE POOR IN SPIRIT – for theirs is the kingdom of heaven.
THOSE WHO MOURN – for they will be comforted.
THE MEEK – for they will inherit the earth.
THOSE WHO HUNGER AND THIRST AFTER RIGHTEOUSNESS – for they will be filled.
THE MERCIFUL – for they will be shown mercy.
THE PURE IN HEART – for they will see God.
THE PEACEMAKERS – for they will be called sons of God.
THOSE WHO ARE PERSECUTED FOR RIGHTEOUSNESS SAKE – for theirs is the kingdom of heaven".
And then Jesus said:
"BLESSED ARE YOU WHEN PEOPLE INSULT YOU AND SAY ALL MANNER OF EVIL AGAINST YOU FALSELY FOR MY SAKE. REJOICE AND BE GLAD BECAUSE GREAT IS YOUR REWARD IN HEAVEN..."

How many of us actually rejoice when we are spoken against? Most of us seek revenge – or at least, would like to.

THREE RELEVANT BIBLE TRANSLATIONS

THE KING JAMES VERSION

The King James Version, as we know it today, was the third English translation. This version was commissioned by King James. The previous two translations in the English language were done by other kings. The first was commissioned by King Henry VIII which was called the "Great Bible". The second English version was called the "Bishops Bible", published in 1568.The puritans differed in the translations because of errors, so King James commissioned a new translation into English. That new translation, the King James Version, started in 1604 and was completed in 1611. The translation was done by 47 scholars of the day, from the Church of England. King James gave strict instructions to have the new version conform to the Ecclesiology and to reflect the Episcopal structure of the Church of England and in the church belief in an ordained clergy. Just as a side note, the Church of England and the Roman Catholic Church are mirror images of one another. The main difference was in whom they designated as infallible and without sin to translate and divide God's Word.

This leads me to believe that some of the new translations are more accurate because they were translated without the bias that King James put on his translation and they incorporate the new information found since the translation of the year 1604. More documents have been discovered, like the Dead Sea Scrolls, which reveal more accurate information. Also, more has been revealed and understood about the Aramaic texts, along with new revelations discovered in archaeology and linguistics I feel that the New International Version or The New King James Version are pretty close in their translations. A statement needs to be made at this point: If God is speaking to you using the King James Version, then use it. It is still God's Word for you.

THE NEW KING JAMES VERSION

In 1975, Thomas Nelson, publisher, commissioned a comprehensive new translation, using 130 respected Bible scholars, lay Christians and church leaders to agree on this new translation. The translation took seven years of comprehensive analysis to synthesize the results for this new translation. This translation is highly respected by the Bible theologians.

THE NEW INTERNATIONAL VERSION (NIV)

In 1965, the NIV was completed. One of the driving forces in this new translation was complete accuracy and a need for a translation that was accurate and yet was worded in the language of the day that the contemporaries spoke. The structure of the original King James Version was translated in the language style of the reign of King James and in the vocabulary of the Church of England. The NIV translation took 10 years and included the studies of a trans-denominational and an international group to assure accuracy without any regional bias. It is also highly respected by the Bible theologians.

Note: All of this information was derived from information gathered from the internet sources on this subject. This is an extremely abbreviated summary of what I have studied. If you are interested, take the time to study the information available.

WHAT COULD ANGER JESUS?

As you read the accounts of Jesus while He walked the earth, you can see a man that was filled with passion for His people. There are accounts where He wept for the sick and even the dead. There is an account where He wept over Jerusalem. There are accounts where He healed the helpless. There are accounts where He did not judge a person's sin but, rather, forgave the sin and said, "Sin no more". His passion for His people was so great that one day he went to the cross to fulfill and pay the blood price required by the Original Law. Even though He did not commit any sin, He chose to offer His blood to pay the blood price for all past, present and future sins to satisfy the requirement of the Original Law. The Original Law – because of Adam's sin, blood must be given to cover all sin. Incidentally, that law has never been repealed, even though some would like to think it has.

Now, knowing all of this – What could cause Jesus to get angry? There are four instances that I could find that caused Jesus to be angry, and there is a common thread that runs through all four. That common thread is a lack of compassion shown by those in authority to His people. The lack of compassion was driven by a need for power and control by using the tools of legalism and hypocrisy.

HYPOCRISY – the pretense of having possessions of feelings or characteristics that one does not possess, especially the deceitful assumption of praiseworthy qualities. Hypocrisy denotes a presumption of admirable qualities such as goodness, sincerity, and honesty by those who actually have the opposite qualities. Since they are unwilling to practice the very qualities that they aspire to, it becomes a practice of dishonesty and deceptiveness. It is a disguise of the real truth and heart of the person. In street talk, it is simply said this way: You ain't what you say you are.

LEGALISM – The Pharisees, as well as many others here on earth today, used the Word of God in a legalist manner to create envy, deception of religiousness and to have control and power over other people's lives. Knowledge of the Scripture can become a tool for self-elevation by making others of less knowledge feel

inferior or inadequate. Knowledge can be a powerful tool to gain control over other people's lives. Eventually, these people become "self-proclaimed doctrinal priests". They ignore the intent and purpose of the teachings of Jesus and turn those teachings into an instrument of destruction. Jesus was all about showing love and humility through giving and forgiving. Power can have contrived force, and this force does not usually lend itself to the acts of giving and forgiving.

Now, let us analyze those three instances:

Jesus was provoked to anger –

Mark 3:1-6 – "Another time he went into the synagogue, and a man with a shriveled hand was there. Some of them were looking for a reason to accuse Jesus, so they watched him closely to see if he would heal him on the Sabbath. Jesus said to the man with the shriveled hand, 'Stand up in front of everyone.'" Then Jesus asked them, 'Which is lawful on the Sabbath: to do good or to do evil, to save a life or to kill?' But they remained silent. He looked around them in anger and was deeply distressed at their stubborn hearts and said to the man, 'Stretch out your hand.' He stretched it out, and his hand was completely restored. Then the Pharisees went out and began to plot with Herodians how they might kill Jesus."

As the record states, Jesus had mercy on a man in need. He felt compassion for the man. Jesus met the man at his most important need. He healed the shriveled hand. The Jewish leaders of the synagogue stood on the law to refuse compassion. They refused to yield to the purpose of the law which made the law a curse to man, rather than a blessing to man. That, in fact, is legalism, and it angered Jesus as is demonstrated in verse 5:

> "He looked around at them in anger and was deeply distressed at their Stubborn hearts and said to the man, 'Stretch out your hand'. He stretched it out, and his hand was completely restored."

Jesus was again provoked to anger. Jesus was provoked to anger by the Pharisees because of their hypocrisy and legalism. Matthew 23:13-37 is commonly referred to as the "Seven woes of Jesus".

> Mark 23:13-37 - "Woe to you, teachers of the law and Pharisees, you hypocrites! You shut the kingdom of heaven in men's faces. You yourselves do not enter, nor will you let those enter who are trying to.
>
> "Woe to you, teachers of the law and Pharisees, you hypocrites! You travel over land and sea to win a single convert, and when he becomes

one, you make him twice as much a son of hell as you are.

"Woe to you, blind guides! You say, 'If anyone swears by the temple, it means nothing; but if anyone swears by the gold of the temple, he is bound by his oath.' You blind fools! Which is greater: the gold or the temple that makes the gold sacred? Therefore, he who swears by the altar swears by it and by everything on it. And he who swears by the temple swears by it and by the one who dwells in it. And he who swears by heaven swears by God's throne and by the one who sits on it.

"Woe to you, teachers of the law and Pharisees, you hypocrites! You give a tenth of your spices – mint, dill and cumin. But you have neglected the more important matters of the law – justice, mercy and faithfulness. You should have practiced the latter, without neglecting the former. You blind guides! You strain out a gnat but swallow a camel.

"Woe to you, teachers of the law and Pharisees, you hypocrites! You are like whitewashed tombs, which look beautiful on the outside but on the inside are full of dead men's bones and everything unclean. In the same way, on the outside you appear to people as righteous, but on the inside you are full of hypocrisy and wickedness.

"Woe to you, teachers of the law and Pharisees, you hypocrites! You build tombs for the

prophets and decorate the graves of the righteous. And you say, 'If we had lived in the days
of our forefathers, we would not have taken
part with them in shedding the blood of the
prophets.' So you testify against yourselves that
you are the descendants of those who murdered the prophets. Fill up, then, the measure
of sin of your forefathers!'

"You snakes! You brood of vipers! How will you
escape being condemned to hell? Therefore, I
am sending you prophets and wise men and
teachers. Some of them you will kill and cru-
cify; others you will flog in your synagogues
and pursue from town to town. And so upon
you will come all the righteous blood that has
been shed on earth, from the blood of righteous Abel to the blood of Zechariah, son of
Berakiah, whom you murdered between the
temple and the altar. I tell you the truth; all this
will come upon the generation.

"O Jerusalem, Jerusalem, you who kill the
prophets and stone those sent to you, how
often I have longed to gather your children
together, as a hen gathers her chicks under
her wings, but you were not willing. Look, your
house is left to you desolate. For I tell you, you
will not see me again until you say, 'Blessed is
he who comes in the name of the Lord'."

Reread this scripture carefully. What could you or I
or anyone else add to Jesus' reaction to the Pharisees and
keepers of the law? It is clear; Jesus has no tolerance for hypocrisy and teachers of the law who do not show compassion for

the less fortunate. That same attitude and passion is shown in Matthew 25:31-46, when Jesus said,
"When you have done it unto the least of these, you have done it unto me".

Jesus has put a command upon His people to help and care for one another and to especially care for the less fortunate and those who need help.

The third record of Jesus being angered was at the temple. There are two accounts of this incidence - Mark 11:15-18 and Matthew 21:12,13.

> Mark 11:15-18 - "On reaching Jerusalem, Jesus entered the temple area and began driving out those who were buying and selling there. He overturned the tables of the money changers and the benches of those selling doves and would not allow anyone to carry merchandise through the temple courts. And as he taught them, he said, 'Is it not written: "My house will be called a house of prayer for all nations"? But you have made it a den of robbers.'

> The chief priests and the teachers of the law heard this and began looking for a way to kill him, for they feared him, because the whole crowd was amazed at his teaching."

> Matthew 21:12,13 "Jesus entered the temple area and drove out all who were buying and selling there. He overturned the tables of the money changers and the benches of those selling doves. 'It is written,' he said to them, "My house will be called a house of prayer", but you are making it a den of robbers."

The temple signifies a place of rest, peace and reverence, not a place of commerce. The church (temple) today is often used as a social center to create perceptions and illusions for social and/or business purposes. Yes, I said business purposes. People can also use the church to gain and give the perception of spirituality. That is called hypocrisy. Because, the presumption is that you are going to church for worship purposes, but the church occasion is used for other purposes. Many times in various churches, I have overheard people discussing and communicating business transactions during a time that should be held for worship or preparation for worship. Maybe you have seen this happen in your church as well, or even worse, you yourself are guilty of the same thing.

A fourth record of Jesus being angered also involved hypocrisy, as well as legalism. It is found in Matthew 15 vs. 1-9 (The Living Bible) –

"Some Pharisees and other Jewish leaders now arrived from Jerusalem to interview Jesus. 'Why do your disciples break the tradition of the elders? They don't wash their hands before they eat!" Jesus replied, 'And why do your traditions violate the direct commands of God. For instance, God's law is to honor your father and mother; anyone who reviles his parents must die.' But you say, 'Even if your parents are in need, you may give their support money to the church instead.' And so, by your man-made rule, you disobey the direct command of God to honor and care for your parents. You hypocrites! Well did Isaiah prophesy of you: 'These people say that they honor me, but their hearts are far from me. Their worship is worthless.

All of us can be guilty of this hypocrisy – using one good act which pleases God to justify overlooking another good act which pleases God more. The Pharisees felt righteous in that they were giving money as an offering to

God. But, they were doing it at the expense of helping their own parents. This angered Jesus to the point of calling them hypocrites. They neglected what was more important for a lesser work. Perhaps there were unresolved issues with their parents which made it easier to help the poor and needy. They might have been justified. Nevertheless, Jesus did not excuse them. In fact, he became very angry with them.

This is an area we can all fall short in. Some may even claim that "Honor thy Father and Mother" is part of the Old Covenant. However, Jesus, who had just ushered in the New Covenant, made it clear that honoring their father and mother came first before honoring and helping others. In writing about what angered God and including this fourth record of Jesus being angered, I saw something for the first time. Jesus was very angry that these Pharisees had not honored their parents. Think with me for a moment. What was the source of Jesus' anger when he drove out the money changers, buyers and sellers from the Temple? He said that His father's house was to be a house of prayer. They had not honored His father. Now, there is a common problem between both of these incidents. – not honoring parents. In the same way that He was angered with the Pharisees for neglecting their parents, He is angry when we do not honor our father and mother. And that honor is not contingent on whether or not they deserve it. I wonder how often we also at times do not honor our parents and so "nullify the word of God." I wonder how often, when we do not honor our parents, that we honor God with our lips but our heart is far from Him?

CONCLUSION: Our Holy Father loves His creations and His people. He showed that love with His Son Jesus at the cross. God sent His only Son to show the only way that man can live in total harmony, and that is through giving and forgiving. Our

Holy Father likes the "real thing". He does not like hypocrisy. God wants passion and compassion over the structure of the law and hypocrisy.

Everybody has a concept and a value and an expectation from God the Father, Jesus the Son and the Holy Spirit. The bigger question is this – What do you think the Trinity's expectation is of you? What is it? I like to keep little phrases in mind to help guide me. One phrase is this – What <u>displeases</u> God the most is not what has been done for the sake of God, but, rather, what has been done for the sake of self. He wants us <u>to give</u> and <u>forgive</u> as a desire to demonstrate our love for Him.

You have had a chance to read and review what has angered Jesus. As you think about your relationship and walk with God, do you have any reason to believe that your walk would provoke anger in our Lord?

WHY DID EVE EAT THE FRUIT OF THE TREE? AND WHY DID ADAM DISOBEY GOD AND EAT ALSO?

If you study the text and the context of why Eve ate the fruit of the tree, it becomes obvious that she ate the fruit of the forbidden tree for her own glorification, edification and her selfish desires. Read Genesis 3:1-7, paying special attention to verse 6.

> "Now the serpent was more crafty than any of the wild animals the Lord God had made. He said to the woman 'Did God really say, "You must not eat from any tree in the garden'?" (2) The woman said to the serpent, 'We may eat from the trees in the garden, (3) but God did say, "You must not eat from the tree that is in the middle of the garden, and you must not touch it or you will die'. (4) 'You will not

surely die,' the serpent said to the woman. (5) 'For God knows that when you eat of it, your eyes will be opened, and you will be like God, knowing good and evil'. (6) When the woman saw that the fruit of the tree was good for food and pleasing to the eye, and also desirable for gaining wisdom, she took some and ate it. She also gave some to her husband, who was with her, and he ate it. (7) Then the eyes of both of them were opened, and they realized they were naked; so they sewed fig leaves together and made coverings for themselves.

It is obvious that Eve was not content with all that Eden had to offer her. She was tempted and fell into the same trap so many of us do. We are not satisfied with all the good things that God has given us. Too often, we tend to desire the things we don't have, rather than appreciate the things that we do have. The serpent tempted her at her weakest point, and that was greed and serving self. Isn't that really true of what we deal with today? Sin is all about us, serving self rather than serving God.

After reading this, there are some general observations that can be made:

1. Satan did not approach Adam. Satan dealt only with Eve concerning eating the forbidden fruit, which would open the door to sin. He did not approach Adam. Satan obviously must have known that Eve had the weaknesses that we previously discussed, so he approached Eve.

2. Eve was evidently the decision maker between Adam and Eve. Eve made the decision to eat the fruit, and Adam went along with her decision. Adam could have chosen not to eat the fruit, but he chose to eat the fruit. Why? Was it because he was trying to gain Eve's favor and approval rather

than God's favor and approval? If that is the case, then that is what caused him to sin. There is a lesson here.
3. Adam must not have had much character and he must have been pretty spineless. He demonstrated that trait just as much as many of us demonstrate the same trait. He demonstrated the fact the he didn't want to accept responsibility for his own decision. He wanted to transfer the guilt of his decision over to Eve. See Genesis 3:11-12 below:

> 11) "And he said, 'Who told you that you were naked? Have you eaten from the tree that I commanded you not to eat from'? The man said, 'The woman you put here with me – she gave me some fruit from the tree, and I ate it'.

Just as Eve tried to blame Satan for her sin, Adam tried to blame Eve and God (indirectly). It is interesting how this scenario has been played out throughout the history of man and God's creation.

CHAPTER 2

INSPIRED THINKING

A TRUE STORY – 10-6-2007

Last Saturday I went to a store looking for a wood-burning fireplace grate. I was met by the owner and a black man in his forties. They did not have a new grate that was suitable, so we looked through the used ones. Through this whole process, my attention was given to this black man who was helping me out, because he was so willing to help and was kind and happy. If you were to look at him, most people would wonder why he was so content and happy since his clothes were old and were not the right size for him. His skin was weathered with deep wrinkles on his face and forehead. He had missing teeth, the four middle teeth on the top and bottom that were very apparent as he smiled. I asked him what his job was and he said, "I do all da hard work for da business place", and then he said, "I works here fo a long time and I happy dat I gots a job". He put the grate in the back of my car. After he did that, I went over and put my arm around his shoulder and said, "I want you to know Jesus loves you". He grinned and grabbed my hand with his hand, which was big and hard with heavy calluses, and said, "Why I know dat. He gots me up dis morning and I wasn't even hungry til I gots up". After that, I hugged him and told him he was my brother in the Lord.

As I was driving away, I thought this man of very little means and virtually no education took me to school! This man showed me that real joy and contentment lie in the heart, not in the things of the world. While he does not possess many things of this world, he does posses the most important thing – to know that God lives in your heart and to be content in all things. This is an example that verifies the Scripture where Paul wrote about being content in all things. Well, I consider this man to have a doctorate (PhD) in what Jesus wants to teach us, and yet he has no possessions or formal education. I consider this man to be my role model and yet he has no worldly influence.

Thank you, Jesus, for revealing Yourself through this man – your servant.

APATHY IN CHRISTIANITY

Hebrews 6 vs. 1-3 – "Therefore, let us leave the elementary teachings about Christ and go on to maturity, not laying again the foundation of repentance from acts that lead to death, and of faith in God, instructions about baptisms, the laying on of hands, the resurrection of the dead and eternal judgment. And God permitting, we will do so."

Apathy is probably the biggest killer of Christianity and the church today. It is a disease that is destroying the church as well as our Christian faith. Most people's Christian experience is confined to the inner walls of the church. Their Christian experience is centered around what is good and necessary for the church property, prestige, programs and the church orga-nizations. The church and its members evolve into an endless religious merry-go-round and it ends up being a waste of time, energy and money. Christians run from one church meeting to another, one bible study to another, one sermon to another. Why do that? They have not done anything with what they have learned from the previous bible studies or sermons. All of this self-focused activity breeds apathy towards what God has prepared us for. God prepared us to go out into the world to spread the gospel of Jesus Christ and to be an example of His loving grace. God was very clear in Hebrews 8 when He said He put within each of us all that is necessary about His basic standard of righteousness.

Also, in Romans Chapter 1, when He said "Even those who have not heard the gospel are held accountable to the sense of right and wrong that God put within them". Also, when Jesus was praying for His disciples and His followers just before he went to the Garden of Gethsemane, he prayed – "I have given them all You have given me, God, so that they would go out into the world to profess my name and to share your standard of righteousness". I believe bible studies should prepare us to do God's will, instead of prepare us for another bible study. The same is true of sermons. Sermons should prepare us to go out into the world, not for the next sermon.

Now, coming back to the Scripture when the writer of Hebrews said, "Therefore let us leave the elementary teaching about Christ and go on to maturity". I believe this scripture is referring to the elementary teaching as those things you already know about bible studies and church activity and sermons. You have done those things many times over. Now "go on to maturity". Go out into the world and make a difference for the cause and glory of Jesus the Christ. Christians, we have the Word of God. We are experiencing His love. We have the answers that the world is looking for. I love following Christ and going out into the world.

At first glance, it would appear that I am blatantly denying the value of bible teaching and sermons. I cannot end this thought process without a clarification of the value of Bible teaching and sanctification through the study of God's Word and revelation through sermons. The Bible is God's last truth given to man. The Bible defines God's standard of righteousness. Let me be real clear on the subject of teaching Bible knowledge and preachers revealing God's truth through sermons. God must have teachers, Bible knowledge and revelation of God's truth through preachers and their sermons. My point is this: teaching, studying and sermons are only the beginning. As this scripture says, if we keep rehearsing what we already know, this process becomes elementary. At some point in time, to become mature, we must apply what we know through the gifts God has given us. May God bless you.

ARE YOU GUILTY?

If you were put on trial for being a Christian, would your friends, your family, your neighbors, your community or the world have enough evidence to conclusively, and without a doubt, prove you are a Christian? While attending a church service or a church event, the church members may have a perception of some kind of evidence, but does anyone else see that evidence outside of this spiritual setting? Witnessing and discussing spiritual things are easy in a spiritual setting, such as a church service or church function, but that is not where it is needed most. Outside of the safety of a spiritual setting is where a person should provide enough evidence to be convicted of being a follower of Jesus – A Christian.

ATTITUDE/GRATITUDE

Gratitude is an attitude. Without an attitude of gratitude, then gratitude cannot be an attitude. It is the attitude of gratitude that minimized the need for favorable circumstances in life for you to find joy and contentment. Without an attitude of gratitude, the price tag of joy and peace and contentment increases without an end. I am convinced that the impact of the circumstances of our life is 90% a perception of those circumstances and 90% of those perceptions start with an attitude – An Attitude of Gratitude.

BELIEVING AND/OR NOT BELIEVING IN GOD

Believe – "accepting something as true". If we analysis this definition and say I accept something as true, then we believe what we accepted as true. So, everybody believes in something. There are those who say they do not believe, or at least believe in, God. My argument to those who say they do not believe there is a God - They actually believe there is a God that they do not believe in. How can they not believe in something that does not exist; therefore, they are acknowledging a God. Everybody has a belief system. Now, a belief must have a basis for what is being believed in. The basis of what is believed then defines and describes what we believe and why we believe in it or do not believe in it. The basis of what we believe comes in one of two forms. One belief system comes from the outside/ inward. What we believe in our mind comes from all of external sensations acting on our body. We only believe what we can see, feel to the touch, hear, etc. I have heard it said "If I cannot taste, touch, hear, or just feel it, then I do not believe it". They will say, "That is why I do not believe in God". If that is the case, they are deprived of the non-feeling things like love, peace, joy, etc. Question: Can a person believe that absolute darkness exists? You cannot believe in darkness if you believe only in what responds to the senses, but darkness has no energy source to respond to the senses and neither does cold. So, if you believe in darkness or cold, you do believe in something that does not respond to the senses. Now, back to the basis of what you believe. Maybe you do believe in some things you do not understand, which leads me to the next, or other, method of believing.

Believing on the things from the outside/in is absolutely true and necessary. However, believing in those non-tangible things that come from the "inside /out" are as real as those things that come from the "outside/in". The truth and belief of being a Christian can seem strange to those who do not believe in God. . For those who <u>do not</u> know God, they cannot feel or experience His touch or presence in their life. Those who truly know God – they can feel and experience His loving touch. It is amazing how that works. That non-tangible feeling from God actually becomes a tangible feeling within a true believer. It becomes so tangible that it feels like your best friend walks with you each moment of the day. I wish so much that the non-believers could know Jesus, so they could feel the non-tangible become tangible in their lives. Oh, if they could only know!

Now, back to believing and non-believing - As for those who claim they do not believe in God, they are only fooling themselves because they have to believe in a God that they do not believe in. What a shame. God created <u>every</u> person out of a love for that person. He has a perfect plan for each person He has created, but by not trusting in the creator, the person is missing out on the joy and peace God has for him. What a shame!

Now, for those who <u>truly</u> believe in God, commit your life to Him and experience the blessing that will come from the inside/out: joy, peace, purpose and contentment. These attributes can exist no matter what comes from the outside, because God will give you <u>inward</u> peace if you totally give yourself to Him.

<u>Outside/in</u> or <u>inside/out</u> – your choice!

BUSY, BUSY, BUSY

Each person has a little world they live within and they are busy, busy, busy. For over 40 years I have been involved in other people's little world. Note: No matter how big they think their world is, it is still a pretty little world. Over the years, I have watched their world get busy, busy, and even busier, and my world has done the same thing. I think that is one of Satan's most effective tools to keep us distracted from God's daily rich blessings by keeping us busy. People are so busily obsessed with acquiring stuff and status that they do not take time to enjoy what they have acquired. What a shame. There is so much mental distress, depression, divorce and discontent because people are focused on what they do not have rather than what they do have. If we would put ALL things on the balance beam to weigh what is good verses what is bad or even how bad it could be, we would easily see how grateful we should be for how good our lives are, especially when we consider how bad it could be. Maybe if we took time to look for what is good that God has already provided, we may not feel the need to be busy, busy busy striving to get more. Maybe all of the problems associated with the stress of trying to acquire more stuff and status would go away if we could learn to be content and appreciate what we already have.

Busy, busy, busy – and why are we so busy, busy, busy? Question: Are we better off for it? **BUSY:**

BEING
UNDER
SATAN'S
YOKE

CAPTIVITY – THE STORY OF JOSEPH
Genesis 35-50

<u>The Captivity of God's Chosen People – the Sons of Israel (Jacob)</u>
How did the twelve tribes of Israel become enslaved in Egypt? Well, their captivity started when they gave control of their lives and financial well being to Egypt. Oh really? How can that be true? Do you remember the story of Joseph? God favored Joseph and that angered his brothers. Actually, it also angered his father Jacob. As the Bible tells it, his brothers sold him into slavery. During the whole time of his slavery, he never forgot his God in all of his activities. Through a God orchestrated series of events, he found favor with the Pharaoh, so the Pharaoh made him ruler of Egypt next to the Pharaoh.

God caused a seven-year drought. God revealed this drought to Joseph prior to the drought, so Joseph stored up all of the grain to last through the drought. <u>Here is where we get into the cause of the problem</u>. The government of Egypt had enough grain, but the sons of Israel did not have grain. <u>So</u>, eventually Israel and his twelve sons gave their lives, fortune and well-being to the authority of the government of Egypt. Mistake! That was the beginning of their captivity. Eventually, they were enslaved by the government of Egypt. It all started when they gave themselves over to <u>A</u> government. Leadership changed, and they were trapped. The price of that mistake lasted four hundred years in captivity. As a side note: God did eventually give them the promised land that He had promised to Israel, but look at the price they paid for not trusting God.

This outline of these events is relevant. Here is how it is relevant: God built the greatest country of all times, the United States of America, on the principal of believing in Him, doing His will and the principal of individual initiative rather than government initiative and control. When God's people – the 12 sons of Israel – gave themselves over to a secular government, they also gave themselves over to ruin and captivity.

Here is the parallel: We, the people of the U.S.A., are giving our well-being control and freedom over to the control of the government, and it can only go one way, and that way is down into captivity. It is coming. All of the great countries – England, Greece, Italy, the Roman Empire, etc., have taken the path that this country, the United States of America, is going. The signs are everywhere, and lately, the biggest sign is in our healthcare system. The government is trying to take our healthcare over to control every aspect of it. THE END IS COMING. The healthcare takeover is just part of what is coming. There is more to come. The government is dismantling our military. WOW. I cannot understand all of this.

Does history have any value? It sure does! It forecasts the future. Actually, the Bible makes a statement about knowing history. The Corinthians asked about the relevance of the old covenant. Paul's response is recorded in I Corinthians 10:1-12:

> "For I do not want you to be ignorant of the fact, brothers, that our forefathers were all under the cloud and that they all passed through the sea. They were all baptized into Moses in the cloud and in the sea. They all ate the same spiritual food and drank the same spiritual drink; for they drank from the spiritual rock that accompanied them, and that rock was Christ. Nevertheless, God was not pleased with most of them; their bodies were scattered over the desert.

> "<u>Now these things occurred as examples to keep us from setting our hearts on evil things as they did</u>. Do not be idolaters, as some of them were; as it is written: 'The people sat down to eat and drink and got up to indulge in pagan revelry'. We should not commit sexual

immorality, as some of them did – and in one day twenty-three thousand of them died. We should not test the Lord, as some of them did – and were killed by snakes. And do not grumble, as some of them did – and were killed by the destroying angel."

"<u>These things happened to them as examples and were written down as warnings for us, on whom the fulfillment of the ages has come</u>. So, if you think you are standing firm, be careful that you don't fall! No temptation has seized you except what is common to man. And God is faithful; he will not let you be tempted beyond what you can bear. But when you are tempted, he will also provide a way out so that you can stand up under it".

Notice again verse 6:

"Now these things occurred as examples to keep us from setting our hearts on evil things, as they did".

Notice again verse 11:

"These things happened to them as examples and were written down as warnings for us, on whom the fulfillment of the ages has come".

The Old Testament is a perfect example of what God does when you obey Him. It is also an example of what happens when we do not obey Him. The story of Joseph is a great example of that principal. We are walking in the footsteps of those who have fallen before us.

One last note: the American Creed was one of the foundational principals of the Government. It goes something like this: I believe in the United States of America as a government of the people, by the people and for the people, whose just powers were derived from the consent of the governed. In the most recent years, that has changed. It now goes something like this: I, the government, believe in the government as a government of the government, by the government and for the government, whose just powers are derived by the consent of the government. Our founding fathers, who gave so much, would be ashamed of the government leaders as they are today.

CHALLENGES

Challenges are vital to life. Challenge is the driving force to inspire cultural, spiritual, business, knowledge, civil and personal growth. As important as challenge is to our culture and personal growth, it is not <u>as</u> important as our <u>response</u> to challenge. Challenges will persist. They are perpetual. The way we respond and react to challenges will determine whether we become victims or benefactors of challenges.

CHOOSING HAPPINESS IS YOUR CHOICE

Life is full of circumstances. Some circumstances we can understand and some we cannot. Some circumstances we will like and some we won't. The reality of life's circumstances is this – they will prevail. The way we deal with them is our choice. If we choose to view life's circumstances from the negative, then we will <u>NOT</u> be happy. If we choose to view life's circumstances from the positive, we can be happy. IT IS OUR CHOICE.

There is an old analogy about a glass being half full or half empty. There are those who see the glass as half empty. They choose to ignore the fact that the glass is half full of blessings and because of that, they miss the joy of the blessings. Then there are those that realize that there is an emptiness there because the glass is half full. That emptiness represents disappointments, sorrows and unfulfilled expectations. They choose to live with all of what that emptiness represents, but they focus on the half full portion of the glass that is full of life's blessings. If it is possible to be happy, they will be happy.

HERE IS THE DEAL: Life's circumstances are by God's design; they will prevail. The way you deal with them is a choice granted to you and to me by God's grace. We do not deserve that choice. That choice is given to us by His grace. Please understand that God wants us to enjoy His blessings. When you look for them, you will be overwhelmed by what you find. Satan will do all that he can to direct you away from God's blessings so that you will have a separation from God. Satan is the controller of sadness, disappointment and sorrow. He is a master of redirecting your thinking from what you have to what you do not have.

DIRECT MY PATH

If you are asking God to direct your path, you must be moving. If you are not moving, how can God change your direction? A person who is not moving has no direction, and, therefore, does not have a basis for change to start a new direction. Keep moving toward what you know as God's righteousness and will for you, and He will move you, direct your path and charter your course to fulfill the calling of your creation. Only then will you find total joy, peace and contentment. This is how, I believe, the martyrs were able to willingly give their lives for the namesake of our Lord Jesus. The following scripture is a good example of the importance of moving so that God can direct your path:

> Isaiah 30:21 - "Whenever you turn to the right or to the left, your ears will hear a voice behind you, saying, 'This is the way; walk in it."

DOES GOD SPEAK TO HUMANS?

Is there a question about whether God speaks to humans? Did God speak to Moses? Did God speak to Mary? Did God speak to Daniel? Did God speak to Abraham? Did God speak to Job? Great men of faith, strong Christians, say God spoke to them. Billy Graham, Franklin Graham, Adrian Rodgers, John Wesley, Steven Olford, and most Bible preaching preachers say that God speaks to them. Christians of a lesser stature also agree that God communicates with them. In fact, it appears to me that God does not speak to those He does not know. If God is not communicating with a person, there is a reason for a great concern.

Scripture reference: John 10:27 – Jesus speaking of his followers,

"My sheep listen to my voice; I know them and they follow me."

EMOTIONALLY INVOLVED

It is easy to become emotionally involved in a circumstance or set of circumstances. Our decisions, based on emotion, are often very bad decisions.

It would be wise to step back, wait for a little bit, think through what is going on and ask yourself, "What would the Lord have me do?" At that point, you would be capable of making a good decision.

EVOLUTION VS CREATION

Evolution/Creation – A television editorial which dispelled the validity of creation and promoted the concept of evolution ignited my thought process.

The fundamental driving force of evolution is survival – survival of the fittest. If we are a product of evolution, then the essence of our existence would be centered around the rudimentary function of survival. The essence of our existence would be to survive, even to the exclusion or extinction of all other elements of life, even animal life, or human life which includes family members. These characteristics are demonstrated in the animal wildlife world. Some animals will eat their own if they have to. Pure evolution does not have to provide for self denial or self destruction, but rather, for self absorption and survival. With this in mind, an interesting question emerges: If we are a function of evolution, where do self denial, compassion, faith trust and commitment even to death come from? The answer to this question is obvious. Evolution does not answer the dynamics of this question; only creation can answer these questions.

At our creation, God put within us the capacity for love, compassion, faith, trust, self denial and commitment even to death. By virtue of our creation, all of us have the potential for these God-given traits. The energy source that dynamically empowers these traits is "God within us" through the Holy Spirit. It is only when we accept a new life through Jesus Christ and repentance for our former life, can we truly commit to something greater than our self.

Evolution of a species? Yeh, right! Only a fool can chase after the illusions of evolution. My simple answer to evolution is this ... Your mother may have been a descendant of a monkey, but my mother was not!

FRUIT OR THORNS

Hebrews 6:7,8 -

"Land that drinks in the rain often falling on it and that produces a crop useful to those for whom it is farmed, receives the blessing of God. But land that produces thorns and thistles is

worthless and is in danger of being cursed. In
the end it will be burned".

The Scripture says: "It rains on the just and the unjust". This
Scripture tells me that God's blessings fall on all of His creation.
Those people who use their blessings to glorify the Lord will
receive a blessing from God. <u>And</u> to those who do nothing
with God's blessings, or bad things with God's blessings, they
are as thorns and thistles. They will be the ones who are considered as worthless and are in danger of being cursed. Once
again, it says, "In the end, it will be burned". What does that
mean? You figure it out.

GUARANTEES

After being in the financial world for thirty-six years, acting
as an insurance broker and a stocks & bonds market-related
broker, I have become acutely aware of all the various risks
and guarantees associated with financial instruments. Here is
a fact about risk-management of investments that needs to be
mentioned: Very few people have even a small clue as to how
to evaluate risk, yet they bet their entire future on risk-invest-
ment instruments they do not understand.

Because of this attention given to risk and guarantees, I
have been able to generalize these principals to life in general.
Below is a discussion of guarantees which is essential for you
to know:

Now, how about GUARANTEES? Note: A guarantee is
only as good as the institution underwriting the guarantee.
Interesting! Now, what is the ultimate guarantee that guarantees all guarantees in the U.S.A.? What is the guarantee
that guarantees our entire way of Life? What is it? Well, it is
our military. If our military becomes weak, we will be invaded
and thrown into captivity. Everything we own, including our
freedom, will be seized and we will be slaves to our captors.

Look at the history of all of the once great-power countries. They are now captives.

Here is my point of concern: It appears that this present regime, our current government officials, is weakening our military. Less and less money is being appropriated to the military and is being re-appropriated to the welfare programs here in the U.S.A. This government is pulling out many of our military bases in very strategic places. This is suicide for the next generation of our citizens. If we lose our military, everything else goes with it. Do you realize how strategic our military is? Most of the world is dependent on our military for their security. If our military goes down, so do most of the other nations' security. There are only two other countries that are secure with their own military, and they are China and Russia. This is serious business.

We are walking in the footsteps of all of those great nations that have fallen before us. Can it be fixed? I do not know, but we must try. How? Quit voting people into office who do not understand, or at least do not care, what they are doing. Secondly, hold your congressmen and president accountable to what is good for the U.S.A. instead of their own need and greed. Write them and call them. Let yourself be heard. Our way of life is coming to an end. There are at least 60% of the people in the U.S.A. who just do not care. I care. Do you?

HEAVEN BOUND? - OR NOT

Question: Does everybody go to heaven as long as they believe they will go to heaven? There seems to be a thought, or belief, that going to heaven is a state of mind. Live any way you want and do anything you want, and that is ok with God as long as you have said a word or two of a profession of faith and believe you are going to heaven. Does it really work that way?

There seems to be a concern by truly born-again Christians, including myself, that far too many people think that being a

Christian is a state of mind, and there are no prerequisites or requisites to enter into heaven. That attitude is simply saying, "If I believe I will go to heaven, I will go to heaven, regardless of how I live or what I do".

Question: Is that what the Bible teaches? I do not think so. At the risk of being judgmental, I am going to question that kind of thinking or philosophy. Note: With what I just said, I am going to qualify that statement. To challenge who is a Christian or not, or who is going to heaven or not, is <u>not</u> my call. Only our Heavenly Father can make that call. However, the Bible calls out a lot of specific indicators of who is truly worthy to wear the name tag of being a Christian and who will and will not enter heaven.

God set up His standards of righteousness that clearly define what God expects and desires of those who call themselves a Christian. He sent Jesus to deliver those standards by being the example while living on earth.

Here is the problem: Man has re-arranged and selectively chosen those scriptures that will justify the life they want to live. In essence, they have redefined what God has called sin and what is <u>not</u> sin. Question: Will that pass the test at judgment time? That is an important question, because at judgment time, our fate is sealed. It is either heaven or hell for eternity. At least that is what the Bible says. All of the schemes that were contrived to justify the way we want live will not matter at judgment time. Heaven or hell and nothing between heaven or hell.

The Shocker – Jesus gave us a shocking reality, at least to those who will <u>not</u> enter into heaven. Jesus is the gate keeper, so to speak. In Matthew 7:13,14, He made this statement:

"Enter through the narrow gate. For wide is the gate and broad is the road that leads to destruction, and many enter through it. But small is the gate and narrow the road that leads to life and only a few find it."

Wow! That is a game changer for those who do not qualify. Essentially, Jesus is saying there are certain requirements which give evidence that we will enter the narrow gate that leads to eternal life. The next question: What are the requirements that give evidence of the eligibility to enter through the narrow gate to eternal life:

Jesus was sent to earth to define those requirements which give evidence that a person is a Christian. Those requirements are referred to as God's standard of righteousness. It is my opinion that the basis for these standards evolve around four principles: 1) Put no other God <u>before</u> our Holy Father, 2) Be a <u>giver</u>, 3) Be a <u>forgiver</u>, and 4) Practice <u>mercy</u>. If we practice these principles, we will show that we love our God and that we love our fellow man and woman. Jesus also gave an insider look at what pleases Him, as it is detailed in Matthew 5:1-2:

> "Now when he saw the crowds, he went up on a mountainside and sat down. His disciples came to him, and he began to teach them, saying:
>
> 'Blessed are the poor in spirit, for theirs is the kingdom of heaven.
>
> Blessed are those who mourn, for they will be comforted.
>
> Blessed are the meek, for they will inherit the earth.
>
> Blessed are those who hunger and thirst for righteousness sake, for they will be filled.
>
> Blessed are the merciful, for they will obtain mercy.

Blessed are the pure in heart, for they will see God.

Blessed are the peacemakers, for they will be called sons of God.

Blessed are those who are persecuted because of righteousness sake, for theirs is the kingdom of heaven.

Blessed are you when people insult you, persecute you, and falsely say all kinds of evil against you because of me',"

Conditions. The next thing to consider is a conditional response that reflects our true and sincere commitment to Him and the rest of His creation. These are evidences of salvation that could be considered requirements, or to fulfill or meet His standard of righteousness. These conditions usually involve the words "if", "therefore", "how can you?", "then", "did or did not", or "thus". (Outlined below are evidences or conditions of our commitment to God):

Of course, the most obvious evidences are the Ten Commandments. By the way, the Ten Commandments not only define the dos and don'ts, but really define the righteous character of God.

Some other examples of the evidences are:

John 14:15 – Jesus said, "If you love me, you will obey what I command".

Colossians 3:12,13 – "Therefore, as God's chosen people, holy and dearly loved, clothe yourselves with compassion, kindness, humility, gentleness and patience."

I Peter 2:19-22 – "For it is commendable if a man bears up under the pain of unjust suffering because he is conscious of God. But, how is it to your credit if you receive a beating for doing wrong and endure it? But, if you suffer for doing good and you endure it, this is commendable before God. To this you were called, because Christ suffered for you, leaving you an example, that you should follow in His steps. "He committed no sin, and no deceit was found in his mouth".

Luke 10:2,3 – "He told them, 'The harvest is plentiful, but the workers are few. Ask the Lord of the harvest, therefore, to send out workers into his harvest field. Go! I am sending you out like lambs among wolves."

I Corinthians 13:4-7 – "Love is patient, love is kind. It does not envy; it does not boast; it is not proud. It is not self-seeking; it is not easily angered; it keeps no record of wrongs. Love does not delight in evil, but rejoices with the truth. It always protects, always trusts, always hopes, always perseveres."

Matthew 7:18-20 – Jesus said, "A good tree cannot bear bad fruit, and a bad tree cannot bear good fruit. Every tree that does not bear good fruit is cut down and thrown into the fire. Thus, by their fruit you will know them."

I John 3:17,18 – "If anyone has material possessions and sees his brother in need but has no pity on him, how can the love of God be in

<u>him</u>? Dear children, let us not love with words or tongues, but with actions and in truth."

Then Jesus made direct commands that bear the same evidence that we belong to God. Examples:

Matthew 22:36-40 – "Teacher, which is the greatest commandment in the Law? Jesus replied, 'Love the Lord your God with all your heart and with all your soul and with all your mind. This is the first and greatest commandment. And the second is like it: Love your neighbor as yourself. All the Law and the Prophets hang on these two commandments."

John 13:34, 35 – Jesus said, "A new commandment I give you: Love one another. As I have loved you, so you must love one another. By this, all men will know that you are my disciples, if you love one another.

John 15:12, 13 – Jesus said, "My command is this: Love each other as I have loved you. Greater love has no one than this, that he lay down his life for his friends."

Luke 11:23 – Jesus said, "He who is not with me is against me, and he who does not gather with me, scatters."

Luke 12:4,5 – Jesus said, "I tell you, my friends, do not be afraid of those who kill the body and after than can do no more. But, I will show you whom you should fear. Fear him who, after the killing of the body, has power to throw you into hell. Yes, I tell you to fear him."

Matthew 16:24-26 – "Then Jesus said to his disciples, 'If anyone would come after me, he must deny himself and take up his cross and follow me. For <u>whoever wants</u> to save his life will lose it, but <u>whoever loses </u>his life for me will find it. What good will it be for a man if he gains the whole world yet forfeits his soul? Or what can a man give in exchange for his soul?"

Matthew 25:45, 46 – Jesus said, "I tell you the truth, whatever you did not do for one of the least of these, you did not do for me. Then <u>they will go away to eternal punishment,</u> but the righteous to eternal life."

CONCLUSION: Is everybody a Christian just because they say so? Is everybody going to heaven because they choose to believe they are? Well, it seems very clear that the gate is truly narrow, and opinions will not get us into heaven. God clearly laid down standards of righteousness that give evidence that we are on the way to heaven. Since heaven is for eternity, and hell is for eternity, it would behoove each of us to seek out our own salvation by studying His word, the Bible, and commit to a prayerful life to seek out His will for our lives. Then go out unto His world to be his ambassador of love, kindness, mercy and to present the gospel for salvation and sanctification. Question: How do the "ifs", "thus", and "therefore" in the scripture apply to your life?

By the way, I have a lot of "ifs", "therefore", and "thus", I am working on in my life too.

HOPE IS ALWAYS THERE

If you feel like life is closing in on you and there is no apparent method or purpose behind the calamity and turmoil in your life; you can still find peace, joy, and purpose. If your problems seem bigger than any solutions, you can still find peace, joy, and purpose. Paul gives us the same encouragement as he did the Corinthians. Read these verses several times. Write them down and refer to them often. May God bless you!

> II Corinthians 4:16-18 - "That is why we never give up. Though our bodies are dying, our inner strength in the Lord is growing every day. These troubles and suffering of ours are, after all, quite small and won't last very long. Yet this short time of distress will result in God's richest blessings upon us forever and ever! So we don't look at what we can see right now, the troubles all around us, but we look forward to the joys in heaven which we have not yet seen. The troubles will soon be over, but the joys to come will last forever.

Paul explains the reality of our dying bodies and explains our hope in spite of our dying bodies in II Corinthians 5:1-9.

> II Corinthians 5:1-9 - "For we know that when this tent we live in now is taken down - when we die and leave these bodies - we will have wonderful new bodies in heaven, homes that will be ours forevermore, made for us by God himself and not by human hands. How weary we grow of our present bodies. That is why we look forward eagerly to the day when we shall

have heavenly bodies which we shall put on like new clothes. For we shall not be merely spirits without bodies.

"These earthly bodies make us groan and sigh, but we wouldn't like to think of dying and having no bodies at all. We want to slip into our new bodies so that these dying bodies will, as it were, be swallowed up by everlasting life. This is what God has prepared for us and, as a guarantee, he has given us his Holy Spirit."

"Now we look forward with confidence to our heavenly bodies, realizing that every moment we spend in these earthly bodies is time spent away from our eternal home in heaven with Jesus. We know these things are true by believing, not by seeing. And we are not afraid, but are quite content to die, for then we will be at home with the Lord. So our aim is to please him always in everything we do, whether we are in this body or away from this body and with him in heaven."

This is one of the greatest hopes ever given to man - second only to the hope of eternal salvation through being born again. If you are unsure of this hope, please call me – 662-397-0452. The hope of salvation is a gift given to us through the blood of Jesus.

HYPOCRITE AND HYPOCRISY

Hypocrisy is the pretense of having possession of feelings or characteristics one does not possess, especially, the deceitful assumption of praise-worthy qualities.

Hypocrisy denotes a presumption of admirable qualities, such as goodness, sincerity, and honesty by those who actually have the opposite qualities. Since they are unwilling to practice the very qualities that they aspire to, it becomes a practice of dishonesty and deceptiveness. It is a disguise of the real truth and heart of a person.

Hypocrite or hypocritical was used 15 times in the Book of Matthew. It was not used as an honorable quality, quite the contrary, it is an indictment. One example of hypocrite is

Matthew 24, vs. 51 – "He will cut him to pieces and assign him a place with the hypocrites, where there will be weeping and gnashing of teeth".

I Need Help

Have you ever been in a situation where you have felt so alone? Where you have felt nobody understood your problems or cared about your problems? Where the problem is bigger than any possible solution? Where even God appears to have abandoned you? You want to make a cry, I Need Help! The problem of being desperate and needing help is not a modern day problem. It dates back to the beginning of time.

The Bible records accounts where people were enraptured by overpowering problems. Some of the problems were psychological, some mental, some self-imposed and some spiritual. Regardless of the reason for the problem, it was still a problem and the Bible records that they made a cry, I Need Help. Those people may not have used those particular words, but that was the intent of their cry, I Need Help. Let us examine a few of those accounts.

NOTE: Before we examine the accounts, it is important to make a distinction of word meanings. The word Lord and Son of David is used many times. Examine the text and meanings of these words.

183

Lord—The word Lord is used in many places and is connected to the name and the person of Jesus. Most people assume that the word "lord" has the same meaning as Messiah, of which it does not. The word "lord" in the Hebrew (the language of the day) meant 'One who has great power or authority'. The word "Lord" was used later in the New Testament as "Master or Owner". At the time of Jesus, they did not know Jesus as their Messiah, but only as one who had power or authority, *a lord*. It was only after the resurrection that Jesus was truly known as the Messiah.

Son of David—It was very common to refer to someone as a descendant of someone else. Since Jesus was the descendant of David it would be natural, and almost expected to refer to him as Jesus, (Son) descendant of David.

Matthew 9 vs. 20-22
A cry for help—Woman with internal bleeding

Just then a woman who had been subject to bleeding for twelve years came up behind him and touched the edge of his cloak. She said to herself, "If I only touch his cloak, I will be healed."

Jesus turned and saw her. "Take heart, daughter," he said, "your faith has healed you." And the woman was healed from that moment.

Here is an example of a woman who had a serious problem for 12 years. I am sure she cried for help for 12 years, but nothing could be done. Finally, she recognized a person with great power and cried out to Jesus as a lord, saying—I Need Help, in a manner of speaking.

Matthew 9 vs. 27-31
A cry for help from two blind men

As Jesus went on from there, two blind men followed him, calling out, "Have mercy on us , Son of David!" When he had gone indoors, the blind men came to him, and he asked them, "Do you believe that I am able to do this?" "Yes Lord," they replied.

Then he touched their eyes and said, "According to your faith will it be done to you"; and their sight was restored. Jesus warned them sternly, "See that no one knows about this." But they went out and spread the news about him all over the region.

This story tells of two blind men that had a problem that was out of their control. They also knew that the solution to their problems could only be dealt with by a lord. They followed Jesus and asked for mercy. Jesus said, "Do you believe that I am able to do this?" They said, "Yes, Lord" referring to the one who has great power—Jesus heard their cry of—I Need Help, and exercised and demonstrated His power by healing them.

Matthew 15 vs. 22-28
A cry for help from a mother whose daughter was demon possessed

A Canaanite woman from that vicinity came to him, crying out, "Lord, Son of David, have mercy on me! My daughter is suffering from a terrible demon-possession."

Jesus did not answer a word. So his disciples came to him and urged him, "Send her away for she keeps crying out after us. "He answered, "I was sent only to the lost sheep of Israel. "The woman came and knelt before him. "Lord, help me!" she said. He replied, "It is not right to take the children's bread and toss it to their dogs."

"Yes, Lord," she said, "but even the dogs eat the crumbs that fall from their masters' table." Then Jesus answered, 'Woman, you have great faith! Your request is granted.' And her daughter was healed form that very hour.

This mother must have been desperate. Can you imagine the hopelessness she must have felt? She also did not know Jesus as the Messiah, but Jesus as a lord. Sometimes when life's circumstances seem so helpless and Jesus the Messiah does not seem to be there, you have to cry out—Lord, I Need Help, just as she did. I Need Help.

Matthew 17 vs. 14-16
A cry for help from a man whose son had seizures

When they came to the crowd, a man approached Jesus and knelt before him. "Lord, have mercy on my son," he said. "He is an epileptic and is suffering greatly. He often falls into the fire or into the water. I brought him to your disciples, but they could not heal him."

Here is an account of a man who seemed to have a problem that was bigger than any known solution. He cried out, "Lord (one who has power) have mercy on my son." He had heard enough to know Jesus was a lord, but wouldn't it have been wonderful if he would have known him as the Messiah? That distinction of Messiah was yet to come.

Many of us know Jesus as Lord and as the Messiah and as Our Savior but even knowing all of this, we can feel so abandoned and alone. Sometimes there's nothing left to do but cry out—I Need Help. Jesus will hear your cry. You may not be able to predict or recognize His response immediately, but He will respond.

Mark 2 vs. 1-9
A cry for help from the friends of a paralyzed man

A few days later, when Jesus again entered Capernaum, the people heard that he had come home. So many gathered that there was no room left, not even outside the door, and he preached the word to them. Some men came, bringing to him a paralytic, carried by four of them. Since they could not get him to Jesus because of the crowd, they made an opening in the roof above Jesus and, after digging through it, lowered the mat the paralyzed man was lying on. When Jesus saw their faith, he said to the paralytic, 'Son, your sins are forgiven.' Now some teachers of the law were sitting there, thinking to themselves, "Why does this fellow talk like that? He's blaspheming! Who can forgive sins but God alone?"

Immediately Jesus knew in his spirit that this was what they were thinking in their hearts, and he said to them, "Why are you thinking these things? Which is easier: to say to the paralytic, 'Your sins are forgiven,' or to say, 'Get up, take up your mat and walk'? But that you may know that the Son of Man has authority on earth to forgive sins..." He said to the paralytic, "I tell you, get up, take your mat and go home." He got up, took his mat and walked out in full view of them all. This amazed everyone and they praised God, saying, "We have never seen anything like this!"

Here is an account where many men recognized the Lordship of Jesus and made a cry for help. I Need Help.

A NOTE ON THE HEALINGS DONE BY JESUS

Jesus did healing freely during his walk on earth to demonstrate the power given to him by His Holy Father. This power was given to demonstrate and to establish His role and position of not only Lord, but also, as a prelude to His ultimate role as the Messiah—The Son of God.

While Jesus walked on earth, He was God/Man. Once He was crucified, He gave up His earthly role and became God/Savior. The method, purpose, function and intention of the healings done as God/Man (while Jesus walked on earth) were done for a different reason than after the resurrection and ascension when He became God/Savior. The act that established Him as the Messiah happened at resurrection and ascension. The event of resurrection and ascension validated all that He taught. One of His major roles was to come as a teacher to reveal the last and ultimate truth that would ever be given to man. **Now**, as for the healings done after the resurrection and ascension as God/Savior, I personally believe from all that I have read and all that I know about the healings done under the new dispensation and the New Covenant, the healings are, for the most part, done for three reasons. The reasons are these:

- Righteousness - knowing what God values as right and wrong and knowing God's will for our life to serve His purpose.
- Holiness - doing God's will for our good and his purpose.
- Intimacy - God wants to have an intimate love relationship with His people.

Jesus did healing freely to demonstrate the power given to Him by the Lord, for the purpose of establishing His role and position as the Messiah - the Son of God. These healings were all done before the resurrection and his ascension into heaven. Healings done after the resurrection and ascension have a whole different purpose, function and designated intention and that is to establish within each of us, the properties of righteousness, holiness and intimacy.

CONCLUSION: The Bible records many, many instances where many people made a cry for help. What I have illustrated is only a few.

I Need Help - Have you ever been there? Are you there now? Does it seem like nobody understands or cares about your hurts. You may be a Christian and you may be wondering, "God, if you loved me, how could you let me suffer like this?" (I wrote a paper titled ***A RATIONALE FOR THE EXISTENCE OF GOOD AND EVIL*** THAT DISCUSSES THIS TOPIC) Well, the answer is not simple, but the answer is sure and absolute. <u>JESUS IS ALWAYS THERE</u>. We may not always feel His presence but He is always there. During the time of His walk on earth, Jesus did a lot of physical, emotional and spiritual healings. He did that to establish His Lordship to help justify Himself as the ultimate role He would assume as Messiah. Those healings were very evident, easy to understand and served the purpose for that time. Jesus is still in the business of healing, but the purpose and the motive may be different.

At this point stay with me while I give a rationale for my next proposition. In the first covenant God came to man and man was required to obey out of duty. When Adam sinned in the Garden, God put a barrier between Himself and man and required a blood offering for redemption of sin. Then God made His first contractual agreement with man through Moses. From there, the Old Testament was established. God chose to use intercessors or ambassadors to communicate with His people, rather than dealing with all of His people on an individual basis. The first covenant (the Old Testament) did not work, so God sent Jesus to earth to be the example and to set the standard for His New Covenant, which is revealed through the New Testament. He also sent Jesus to introduce the Holy Spirit. Because of this, God's role and relationship with man changed. In the Old Covenant, God conquered through wars as a method to demonstrate His authority, power and as a discipline tool for His people. Since none of this worked, He changed His method. God did an amazing thing then, He sent Jesus. Instead of keeping a barrier between Himself and man, God stepped toward man and became very intimate with man through Jesus and used the blood of Jesus to cover the sin debt. God stepped toward man again and gave Himself to live within man through the power of the Holy Spirit and now He dwells within us in the form of the Holy Spirit. As I said, under the Old Covenant, He conquered by war. Now under the New Covenant, He conquers by love through giving and forgiving.

Next Proposition—Please consider all of the above as a rationale for a new thought process. <u>The events and circumstances we as humans view as problems may in fact be the very mechanism that God can use to serve his purpose to fulfill His plan for the good of mankind</u>. Remember, we as humans have a finite mind and God doesn't. We as Christians must come to see that God is not part of our plans, but rather Christians are part of His plan.

Let me give you an example of how a person can fulfill God's plan and purpose through the suffering and even death of a loving and privileged person. This person made a tremendous impact on the lives of countless other people. My mother died in a very slow death process. She died at age 58 from cancer. She never complained and was always concerned about the well being of others during her whole dying process. The way she handled this dying process and eventually her death, impacted my life beyond measure and did the same for countless others. The witness of her life has rippled down through two other generations. I would venture to say it altered the lives of hundreds and maybe even thousands. Did she suffer? Yes - very much. Did she have pain? Yes? - very much. Did she complain? No - not that I can remember She was a born-again Christian and she knew her witness had a greater value than her own life. Has God used her pain and suffering for His greater purpose? Yes, yes, yes. Her flesh may be dead, but her memory lives on.

Look at what happened to Jesus for the sake of our Holy Father's plans. Look at John the Baptist. Look at all of the prophets. Look at all of the disciples. They all suffered greatly and they died for the sake of our Holy Father. Now, let us consider our cries. Most of the time our cries, I Need Help, are for the sake of our self. Most of the time our cry should be How can I Help?, rather than I Need Help or our cry should be I Need Help TO DO YOUR WILL. Jesus is still in the business of helping and healing. It may not always come in the form we think we want or understand. Jesus is still in the business of healing. It may not be in the form that we want. Remember, Jesus will do what is necessary to serve all of His creation; Jesus will do what is necessary to refine our righteousness and holiness so that we might serve Him. A lot of times that involves suffering and people do not like suffering.

Remember the next time we make that cry I Need Help, let's try three more words—To Serve You.

If you are not a Christian, just make the cry I Need Help. God will help you because He created you and He loves you and He wants you to be a part of His glorious plan so that you can live in glory for eternity.

ISLAM/MUSLIMS

According to the Islam faith, there are two angels that preside with a Muslim - an angel on the right shoulder and an angel on the left shoulder.

The angel on the right shoulder records all the good that he does during the day. That includes all their prayers and rituals etc.

The angel on the left records all the bad things that he does during the day. At the end of his life he may or may not be able to go to the Promised Land. Allah will weigh all measures of workers and make a call on his eternal destiny

There is an exception to the disposition of his works. If he commits Jihad he automatically goes to the Promised Land, no matter how good or bad his life was.

Note: This is not something I have read from either the Orthodox or Reformed Koran. This is what I heard a former Muslim converted to Christianity, He was once in the higher order of the Muslim belief system. If this is true, it goes a long way to explain why there are so many suicide bombings. Jihad becomes a way to redeem a life that was non-compliant to Muhammad's standards.

IT IS ALL ABOUT ME

Most everybody's basis of measurement concerning reality and identity is based on the world's concept of "It is all about me". When you consider our concept of the world, our reality, and identity of all these experiences is subject to all of our accumulations of our experiences. The larger the experience base we have the easier it is to comprehend and deal rationally with the new and unknown circumstances that life has to offer and places in our pathway. The larger our life circumstances information base provides a way for us to minimize the amount of fears and apprehensions that we run across in our life processes. Our whole basis of measurement comes down to the point of our own reference to these life experiences. Without Jesus Christ, it becomes evident our whole rational being is centered on me and my whole life experiences. Jesus can only turn those life experiences into something that is all about Him and not about me.

How does our belief system through Christianity separate itself from other belief systems? It comes down to this. One of the hardest things to accept and commit to is the fact it requires us to not think about self; to not think about me. But Jesus said we must think about others and we must die to self. All other religions are ultimately enhancing oneself in one way or another. It comes back to the driving force that is within us that deals with the question, "Is my belief system all about me?" or "Is my belief system centered on the premise Jesus proposed, my life is about something other than myself."

C. S. Lewis – The Problem of Pain. This is an interesting book and revealed many new observations. Here is an observation I came up with: Among other things, he so amply pointed out and gives an irrefutable case that we have no rights of expectation from others regardless of real or perceived transgressions that were committed against us. We have no choice but to give and forgive. In the study of the life of Jesus, what did he do to deserve the vengeance of man's sin? Nothing. His life was lived in perfection. Yet, Jesus took the transgression and the guilt for all of our sins He was not guilty of. He was able to go to the cross and accept and pay for these sins. The world would say "Why should you pay for these sins; you did not commit them?" But Jesus would say He was born according to this purpose. Jesus was a perfect model of a carnet state dealing with carnet feelings that involved pain and emotions and He demonstrated in this carnet state an incarnate power by the nature of what He did for us and for His Holy Father. He did this to show and reveal the great message His Father wanted Him to show and that is the great act of giving and forgiving. Jesus' life demonstrated the only possible way that man can live in total harmony and that is for each of us to learn and to know and to exercise unconditional giving and forgiving. His life became the model of this principle.

The interesting facts about the principles of giving and forgiving are this: Every belief system would agree to the fact that if people could learn how to give and forgive unconditionally that man could live in total harmony. Actually, I am to understand that the Jewish religion believes that the principles taught by Jesus Christ are the most pure and perfect principles given to mankind. God revealed His perfect principle to man so that man would have a way to live in total harmony. Jesus became the messenger of that principle. For the life of me, I do not understand why people do not recognize that the messenger came from the same common Holy Father that everybody agrees that exists.

IT IS O.K. TO BE DIFFERENT

Marketing will try to persuade you that you must look a certain way and act a certain way in order to be normal. When you buy into that concept, you will tend to buy the products or services that they offer to make you "fit in" to that concept, thus making you feel normal. Normal is o.k. if your life goal is to be normal. However, not all people desire to be normal. Actually, being normal and fitting in is not what they think about. They think outside the box of "being normal" and actually accomplish abnormal feats. It is not that they are trying to be abnormal, but their God-given inspirations and aspirations cause them to be abnormal. Examples of these people are Thomas Edison, Alexander Graham Bell, Albert Einstein, Isaac Newton and, most of all, Jesus Christ.

Maybe being abnormal should not be so abnormal. If you are abnormal, do not worry about it. Being abnormal is normal if you are with other abnormals. Jesus loves the abnormals too.

JESUS, ARE YOU READY FOR THIS?

This question has a big bearing on what we celebrate as Christmas. The Scriptures say Jesus was with God in the beginning. Putting that in perspective, God the Father may have asked Jesus, "Are You ready for this?" Why would God the Father have asked that question? God the Father provided a way for man to live with man and God the Father in total harmony, but man disobeyed and perverted God's plan of a harmonious co-existence. Because of man's sin toward God the Father and His plan, God the Father provided a way for man to re-acquire a harmonious relationship with Himself. The price tag of that relationship was the shedding of BLOOD. (By the way, God set the standard of shedding blood for man's sin in the Garden of Eden). God the Father decided to provide the redeeming blood through His son Jesus. After the decision was made to send Jesus to earth, my mind's imagination can see God the Father asking Jesus, "ARE YOU READY FOR THIS?"

Are you ready to leave a perfect heaven to go to an imperfect world of selfish human beings?

Are you ready for your flesh to feel the pains of the flesh?

Are you ready for man to celebrate your birth (at Christmas) and then celebrate Your death on the cross (at Easter)?

Are you ready to set the standards of righteousness as I, God the Father define them?

Are you ready to show by example how men can live in total harmony through unconditional giving and forgiving?

Are you ready to destroy religiosity used for power, pride and prestige?

Are you ready to challenge the institution of the church – the church of that day which had evolved and manipulated and re-construed God's perfect plan in order to serve their own organization and personal interests? (By the way, Jesus is here to challenge the churches of today for doing the same).

Are you ready for Palm Sunday when you will be greatly praised and shortly after will be mocked and shamed by false accusations and lies?

Are you ready to be abandoned by your disciples when you need them most?

Are you ready to stand trial and be sentenced to death for what you did not do?

Are you ready to be struck with whips, beaten with rods until your flesh is so mutilated that you cannot be recognized as who you once were? And are you ready to wear a crown of thorns?

Are you ready to be hung on the cross with nails through your hands and feet until you die?

Are you, THE KING OF ALL KINGS, ready to be mocked throughout the whole process? It will start with Christmas day. Are you ready for that?

Are you ready for me to forsake you before you die because of the sin that will be cast upon you?

Are you ready for the spear to be thrust into your ribs so that the blood price will be paid forever to cover all of man's past sins, present sins and future sins?

Are you ready to be buried in a tomb and in three days rise again?

Are you ready to destroy Satan's power over man?

Are you ready to come back to me, God the Father, and prepare a place for those who believe in Me through You and are willing to live by the standards of righteousness that you established while you were on earth?

Are you ready to live with those who are in heaven?

"Jesus, are you ready for this"? Because it will all start on CHRISTMAS DAY. Christmas day is the day when man will celebrate your birth. After that, all of these other events will follow. "Once again, Jesus, are you ready for this"?

WHAT DO YOU THINK JESUS' ANSWER WAS? Thank you, thank you, thank you, Lord Jesus for saying YES!!!!

JESUS – KNOCKING AT THE DOOR

After the fall of man in the Garden of Eden because Adam and Eve ate of the forbidden fruit, man became dirty with sin, so God cast them out of the Garden. In doing so, He also severed His personal relationship with man. Man would remain eternally dirty. However, God gave man a way to be cleansed of man's sin. The method of being cleansed from his sin was with the blood of a spotless animal. Eventually, Jesus became the sacrifice to provide the blood to cleanse men of their sin.

According to history in the Old Covenant, God created a DUTY or transactional relationship with man. Essentially, God dealt with man by setting up many, many DUTY rules, and His agreement was this – if you do this or that, I will bless you or not bless you. As it says in Hebrews, the DUTY covenant (the first covenant) did not work. So, He sent Himself to earth through His Son Jesus, the Christ, to reestablish a new and personal relationship covenant that was not based on a DUTY driven relationship, but a DESIRE driven relationship.

In the first covenant, God came to man through the prophets and through appointed men. Everything about His relationship with man in the first covenant was DUTY driven and somewhat impersonal. God exchanged His first covenant with man. He created a new covenant. Where the old covenant was DUTY driven, the new covenant is DESIRE driven. The new covenant required man to come to God on a DESIRE basis through His son Jesus. This is explained in detail in the book Something to Consider of which I am the author.

With all of that being said, there are four scriptures that refer to a calling by Jesus to man for a personal relationship where man must come to Jesus with a desire to serve Him. All four scriptures deal with a DESIRE relationship and a DESIRED commitment. See what these scriptures mean to you.

> Matthew 7:7-8 - "Ask and it will be given to you; seek and you will find; knock and the door will be opened to you. For everyone who asked receives; he who seeks finds, and to him who knocks, the door will be opened."

> Matthew 7:12 - "In everything, do to others what you would have them do to you, for this sums up the Law and the Prophets." Notice this relationship – Jesus said, "you knock and the door will be opened."

Now, notice the condition, "In everything, do to others what you would have them do to you."

You knock and come with a desire to worship Him. Whenever you knock, there is a condition. Then, in verse 12, He defines the term or conditions that are required when you come to Him after knocking on the door. "In everything, do to others what you would have them do to you, for this sums up the Law and the Prophets." Notice: A relationship with Jesus requires us to give up our selfish desires in order to serve others in His name.

> Luke 11:5-10 - (5) "Then He said to them, "Suppose one of you has a friend, and He goes to him at midnight and says, 'Friend, lend me three loaves of bread, (6) because a friend of mine on a journey has come to me, and I have nothing to set before him.' (7) Then the one inside answers, 'Don't bother me. The door is already locked, and my children are with me in bed. I can't get up and give you anything.' (8) I tell you, though he will not get up and give him the bread because he is his friend, yet because of the man's persistence, he will get up and give him as much as he needs. (9) So I say to you: Ask and it will be given to you; seek and you will find; knock and the door will be opened to you. (10) For everyone who asks receives; he who seeks finds, and to him who knocks, the door will be opened."

Jesus is asking for a DESIRED relationship with Him by asking us to knock on His door. Let this be clear – in this verse, He is not knocking; we must knock. He goes a step further by asking us to pursue Him. Notice verse eight. Perseverance – "yet because of the man's persistence, he will get up and give him as much as he needs." Jesus says, "pursue me on my terms, and I will give you what you need." He wants us to DESIRE to have a personal relationship by having us pursue Him on His terms or conditions. WOW!

> Revelation 3:19-22 - (19) "Those whom I love I rebuke and discipline. So be earnest, and repent. (20) Here I am! I stand at the door and knock. If anyone hears my voice and opens the door, I will come in and eat with him, and he with me. (21) To him who overcomes, I will give the right to sit with me on my throne just as I overcame and sat down with my Father on His throne. (22) He who has an ear, let him hear what the Spirit says to the churches."

Notice the predisposition in verse 19 - "Those whom I love I rebuke and discipline. So be earnest, and repent." This is a very interesting verse. Jesus separates those who could be eligible by the word "those" – meaning not everybody will qualify – only "those". Read it again. "Those whom I love I rebuke and discipline." There is another discussion which I won't get into. If you are not being rebuked and disciplined, does He really love you? That is a question that I will tackle later in another article.

Jesus said he" stands at the door and knocks", but He also said we must open the door, which is a statement of desire to have a relationship on our part. Notice, there is a post disposition in verse 21 "to him who overcomes, I will give the right to sit with me on my throne." God requires a commitment to have a relationship with Him, and that is to "overcome sin". Opening the door is only the first step. What follows is more important.

Luke 13:22-30 - (22) "Then Jesus went through the towns and villages, teaching as He made His way to Jerusalem. (23) Someone asked Him, 'Lord, are only a few people going to be saved?' He said to them, (24) 'Make every effort to enter through the narrow door, because many, tell you, will try to enter and will not be able to. (25) Once the owner of the house gets up and closes the door, you will stand outside knocking and pleading, 'Sir, open the door for us.' But He will answer, 'I don't know you or where you come from.' (26) Then you will say, 'We ate and drank with you, and you taught in our street,' (27) But He will reply, 'I don't know you or where you come from. Away from me, all you evil doers!' (28) There will be weeping and gnashing of teeth, when you see Abraham, Isaac and Jacob and all the prophets in the kingdom, but you yourselves thrown out. (29) People will come from east and west and north and south and will take their places at the feast in the kingdom of God. (30) Indeed, there are those who are last who will be first, and first who will be last."

What can I say about verse 25? "Once the owner of the house gets up and closes the door, you will stand outside knocking and pleading, 'Sir, open the door for us.' But He will answer, 'I don't know you or where you come from.' Jesus is making a very definitive statement. In this illustration, Jesus is implied as the owner of the house. The house represents the Kingdom of Heaven. The scripture says that once the door closes, all of the knocking on the door will not allow you to enter. A person can keep knocking, but it will not matter. I believe there is an explanation of why the door remains closed.

He gave Himself to us in every way and yet there are those who create their own god by manipulating the scripture to suit their desires and needs. It is possible to fool the people around you, but you cannot fool God. This practice of manipulating the scriptures is done by so many that are wearing the Christian label of Christianity. They wear that label of Christianity, not for the purpose of serving the Lord, but they are really wearing that Christianity label to serve their own selfish purpose. Actually, Jesus said only a few will get into heaven. The gateway, or door, is narrow because only a few are willing to serve Him on His terms. Jesus knows the foolish games people play with His name. Saying one thing and doing another is called hypocrisy. God hates hypocrisy. Now, back to the scriptures. Read verses 26 through 30 again – then comes the judgment. ARE YOU READY FOR THAT? ARE YOU READY FOR THAT?!!!

Isn't this interesting? The rest of eternity depends on an understanding of a "knock on the door of Jesus". These verses are used so often to sell religion instead of establishing a relationship with God through Jesus. That relationship requires us to serve Him as His ambassadors by serving Him rather than serving ourselves. WE CAN FOOL EACH OTHER; BUT WE CANNOT FOOL GOD.

JESUS UNDERSTANDS

When Jesus was here on earth, he was both divine and human. Yes, Jesus was HUMAN. In fact the scriptures say that "He did not deny his humanity". And, being human, He suffered as we do and He was tempted by our temptations, but without sin. That is why the book of Hebrews calls Jesus our "sympathetic high priest". Below are listed some of the ways in which Jesus suffered while on earth. These were taken from a ministry website.

JESUS UNDERSTANDS.
The last three years of his life, He was homeless.
His message was rejected.
His family thought he was crazy.
He endured gossip and slander.
He was shamed publicly.
His theology was mocked.
He stood face to face with the devil and endured all of his demonic tricks and temptations.
He endured periods of hunger and thirst.
His disciples didn't get it.
He was rejected by the very ones He came to save.
His disciples all left him.
One of his disciples sold him to be killed for pocket change.
He was filled with anxiety and despair in the Garden of Gethsemane.
He endured suffering for righteousness sake.
HE ENDURED COMPLETE AND UTTER SEPARATION FROM GOD SO THAT YOU WOULD NEVER, EVER, EVER HAVE TO!
YES, JESUS UNDERSTANDS!
Author Unknown

LEARNING FROM MY DOGS - 2010

If I look for it, I can learn from almost anything and every-thing, especially my dogs. Each morning I get up at 5:00, eat my breakfast, read the paper, and then go for a two-mile walk with my two dogs. It is the greatest time of the day because I can enjoy God at His greatest moment – nature. The second great thing about this time is that it allows me to think and meditate and watch my two dogs.

Okay, so what did I learn today? Well, it came from observing my dogs, especially the younger dog, Duke. Feisty, my 14 year-old rat terrier has already taught me about every-thing I already know; at least he thinks so! Now, back to Duke - When I got him out of his kennel, he could not control his enthusiasm as he jumped all over me. Wow. What did I learn? No matter what happened yesterday, today is a new day and he was excited about it. He was anticipating good things and was preparing himself for a good day. Guess what? He is prob-ably going to find what he is looking for. Secondly, as we were walking, I noticed he was eagerly looking in all directions, as though he did not want one thing to escape his attention. He lunged in each direction as if he thought there was something he could get involved in. It seemed as though he wanted to be involved in each and every event that was happening. Wow! He was living life with an expectation that something good was going to happen and he wanted to be part of it. That would be a great lesson to learn.

It is my observation that so many people are depressed and miserable because they <u>are not</u> involved with an expec-tation to be involved in all the good things that life has to offer. So many times, they are not in the good game, but rather, standing on the sidelines licking the wounds of past or present hurts. Duke taught me that I cannot change the past so <u>do not</u> let the past control the moment of today and the hope of tomorrow. Probably, Satan's best tool is to steal the joy of today and the hope of tomorrow is to keep a person angry and bitter about the hurts of the past. The only way to steal Satan's power of anger and bitterness is to practice total forgiveness. It is absolutely the only way to release Satan's control over a person's life. How do I know this? Well, God Himself said so throughout the Scriptures. It is also my observation that when people pursue life with a great expectation of good, like Duke does, they usually find what they are looking for.

Learning from my dogs - Yes, I can generalize my observa-tions from my dogs and learn from them. But, learning without applying what I have learned has no value. Yes, I am going to apply these lessons because I want the joy of today and the hope of tomorrow.

LIFE IS LIVED BY EACH MOMENT

On Thursday, 2-7-08, I woke up at 4:30 and did my usual thing. Went to the Wellness Center at 5:00. Worked out until 5:45 and went home. I went to work. Had a highly- active and fast-moving day at work. I had fun. I got home at 5:00. I noticed some tightening in my chest. Then it happened. I could not breathe and it felt like my heart was pounding out of control. By 6:30, I was in the hospital. Now I have a serious heart problem. Three days later I went home to live an altered lifestyle. WHY AM I TELLING YOU THIS? Here is the reason: If there are high priority things in your life that need to be done and you are procrastinating or waiting for the right time to do it, you could be making the biggest mistake of your life and everybody else's life that you affect. My advice to you is—- Do not wait. Thursday morning and Thursday at 5:00, all was great. I did my usual things that I do and had a great day. Over a one-hour period of time, things went from great to the potential of death or disability. THINK ABOUT IT – just one unexpected hour.

Now, here is my concern for you based on this life-altering experience: I have questions for myself and for you.

1. If you were to die today, would you go to heaven or hell? Our soul is eternal. Our flesh will die, but our soul lives on. Where will your soul be? In glory or in agony? If you cannot answer "in glory", if you are unsure where your soul will reside, call me at 662-397-0452, 662-844-5307 or 662-844-7599. I want to talk to you about this question.
2. If you died today and had the chance to reflect back on your life, what would you do differently? Today is

the day to make the adjustment; tomorrow may not be here for you.

3. If you were to die today and had a chance to look at the world through the eyes of Jesus and you could hear the prayers coming to Him – If you could feel His passion for the unsaved and for the people that are considered the least by social and economic standards – If you could feel His hurt for the hurt of His people – If you could assume the role and passion of Jesus and then evaluate how you have used the resources He has given to you – would you use those resources He has given to you in the same way? These resources were given to elevate God among men, not to elevate man's self among men. If you could see lost souls and did nothing, how will you answer that question when you are asked? If you could see acute hunger or if you could see the naked or if you could see those in prison, and did nothing – how are you going to answer that question? If you could do it over again, would you choose to live your life the same way, or would you choose to live your life a different way? Would you see Jesus' people through His eyes of passion, glory and pain? Or, would you remain cold to the heart of Jesus? Answer: You/I are still alive and are given the power to make those choices. We have that power of choice today, but some day that power will be taken away and then there are the consequences.

4. Has your life been the example that you would want you're your family to follow? Have you unconditionally loved your wife/husband and kids or grandkids? If you were to die, are you happy with the example of your life for them to follow? How about your friends and community? How was your example with them? Have you prepared to take care of your family financially if you were no longer here. The capitalistic system we

live under is a cold and cruel survivor system. You will benefit from that system or you will be a victim of it.

These are things that I have had to consider. Will you consider these things? I have come to know that in most cases, we are a product of our own choices. I have also come to understand that maybe the greatest <u>power</u> we possess is in the power of choice. There is no power in our life that is greater than the power we have to make choices, and someday, when we die, that power will be taken away and the consequences of our choices are fixed and they will prevail. The power of choice is great. Let me remind myself and you that the power of choice we exercise with regard to our relationship with Jesus Christ have eternal consequences. Those consequences will be glorifying or terrifying to each of us. THIS IS SOMETHING TO CONSIDER

LIMITATIONS – NO SUCH THING
II Corinthians 12:6-10

My daughter Lisa sent me this quote –"Do not use your limitations as an excuse for avoiding what God calls us to do". That is a profound statement. I find myself saying, "Lord, I cannot do that because....." In working with other Christians, I hear constantly – "I can't do what God has called me to do because————- (fill in the blanks). Note: All that we call limitations is God's method of doing work for Him. Question: Did God create each of us to be just what we ARE. He knows everything about us – our strengths and weaknesses. There is nothing about us that God considers a weakness or a limitation. He made us and knows us. What we consider our weakness or limitation can be the very thing that God will show His strength through. Paul came to understand and realize that God would use him in his weakness, not his strength and

concluded that "I will boast in my weakness to glorify the Lord."
– II Corinthians 12:6-10.

> "Even if I should choose to boast, I would not
> be a fool, because I would be a fool, because I
> would be speaking the truth. But I refrain, so
> no one will think more of me than is warranted
> by what I do or say.

> "To keep me from becoming conceited because
> of these surpassingly great revelations, there
> was given me a thorn in my flesh, a messenger
> of Satan, to torment me. Three times I pleaded
> with the Lord to take it away from me. But he
> said to me, 'My grace is sufficient for you, for my
> power is made perfect in weakness.' Therefore
> I will boast all the more gladly about my weak-
> nesses, so that Christ's power may rest on me.
> That is why, for Christ's sake, I delight in weak-
> nesses, in insults, in hardships, in persecutions,
> in difficulties. For when I am weak, then I am
> strong."

Question: Is it really our self-perceived or self-imposed limitations, or just an excuse to serve self rather than serve the
Lord? To serve the Lord requires a big commitment - a commitment that may cause hardship and suffering and inconve-
nience. The scripture is very clear that to serve the Lord will
cause you to carry your cross. And the cross is a symbol of
pain and torture. It is so natural and easy to use the excuse
of limitations to avoid the pain of the cross that is required to
serve the Lord. God does not see your conveniently perceived
limitations as a reason to not do what He has called you to do.
Actually, He may be calling you to do what He is calling you to
do because of your perceived limitations. Limitations? Nope;

there are none!! THE THING AT QUESTION IS YOUR DESIRE TO SERVE THE LORD, NOT YOUR ABILITY TO SERVE THE LORD.

People, we must realize we are only here on earth for a brief time. After our heart beats for the last time, we transfer from here to eternity, and then comes the judgment. The only thing that will be remembered is what you did for the Lord, not what you did for self. Are you ready for the judgment?

LOVE IS AN ACTION VERB

A verb denotes action. If a verb is used in a sentence, some kind of action is implied or expected. If a verb is used with no action, it is a misuse of the word. With that in mind, consider the use of a verb that is so frequently used—- I love you. The word "love" in that sentence is a verb that requires or implies an action. If you say "I love you" but do not do the actions necessary to demonstrate what you say, then the words are only words with no true meaning.

If you tell somebody - "I love you" – please remember they are anticipating a demonstration of what you said. If you <u>do not</u> give the demonstration of love, it can be confusing, destructive and frustrating.

Jesus gave the greatest demonstration of "I love you" when he chose to go to the cross and pay for your sin debt. By the way, it would be good to thank Him daily for going to the cross for you.

WHEN YOU SAY "I LOVE YOU", YOU HAVE ALSO MADE A COMMITMENT.

Consider what the Lord has to say about this subject in I John 3:17, 18:

"But if someone who is supposed to be a Christian has money enough to live well and sees a brother in need, and won't help him – how can God's love be within him? Little children, let us stop just saying we love people, let us really love them and show it by our actions."

MISSION WORK AND GOD'S CALL FOR AMBASSADORS

All of creation is justified by the first four words in the Bible: "IN THE BEGINNING GOD".

Question: Why does God want missionaries, ambassadors and churches?

A. History

5. God's creation and the Garden of Eden experience.

    f) God created all things, Genesis 1 and 2.
    g) God created man and woman, Genesis 1 and 2.
    h) God wanted to love and be loved, so He gave man an option to show or not show his love – the forbidden fruit, Genesis 2: 17-17.
    i) They knew their nakedness so God provided an animal skin for cover (first blood in the Garden of Eden would, forever, be the cost of a relationship with God). Hebrews 9, specifically verses 15 and 22.
    j) God banished Adam and Eve from the Garden of Eden. Genesis 3:23, He guarded the way back in with a flaming sword. Genesis 3:24.

6. God changed His relationship with man.

    c) God separated Himself from man and would never DIRECTLY communicate with man except through a mediator (prophet), and sin would never be forgiven except through the giving of blood.

d) Man desired and needed a relationship with his creator. That desire and need never went away. At birth, we are born of flesh and soul. The flesh desires freedom from God and our soul desires a relationship with God. Flesh – all about me. Soul – not about me but God.

7. Study the bible history of how God communicated with man.

    c) Abraham and Moses – God spoke to His people through Abraham and Moses.

    d) The Prophets – Daniel, Joseph, Habakkuk, Nehemiah, Solomon, David, Jeremiah, Isaiah, Malachi and many more. God did not communicate directly with man except through a human mediator. The Jewish faith still teaches this same principle and the Roman Catholic Church practices the same principle to a large extent since the Pope determines truth and none truth. Study the accounts of the prophets.

8. Man could not look upon God, Hebrews 9:1-10.

    c) Atonement of sins – a priest, at a specific time and under specific conditions, could enter the Holy of Holies, the Ark of the Covenant, for atonement.

    d) Moses, at Mt. Sinai, could not look upon God, only upon a burning bush.

B. Jesus became the mediator of the New Covenant. Hebrews 9:15. The Old Covenant relationship with man did not work. Hebrews 8, I Corinthians 10:4-3, Galatians 3:15-25, Hebrews 1:16. So:

9. In the Old Covenant, God had a duty relationship with man.

    b) God has all kinds of laws. He told man what to do, how to do it and when to do it. He conquered through strength and wars. He showed His majesty through Solomon's Temple.

10. In the New Covenant, God changed His relationship from duty driven to desire drive. Instead of conquering by might and wars, He conquers through love, giving, and forgiving.

11. God's relationship with man changed and so did His method of communicating with man.

    f) Abraham and Moses are dead. The prophets are dead, and there with be no more prophets.
    g) One method of God's communication with man is now through us, His chosen people. We are His actions and voice. We are His ambassadors, His evangelists, His kindness, His mercy, His hand and feet of good works, His teachers of the standards of His righteousness and His example of giving and forgiving.
    h) Another method of communication is through the bible. The bible is the last truth given to man. The bible, which is the word of God, is the sword that separates God's truth from Satan's lies. We must have the weapon (the sword of the Spirit) which is the Holy Bible to be part of our armor of protection.

i) Prayer is method of communication. The most intimate relationship with God you will ever have is through prayer. Your intimacy with God, your knowledge of God and His plans for your life is only as strong as your intimate prayer with him.

j) Lastly, the most important method of communication comes from within. After we accept Jesus as our Savior, the scripture says that the Holy Spirit enters in. As Jesus' time on earth came to a close, He told his disciples, "I have much more to say to you, more than you can now bear. But, when He, the spirit of truth comes, He will guide you into all truth. He will not speak on His own; He will speak only what He hears, and He will tell you what is yet to come." John 16:12-13; the bible also tells us that when we do not know what to pray, the Holy Spirit prays for us according to the **will of God.**

12. Jesus knew He was sent by His father to die on the cross for our sins, but He also knew that he was sent to establish God's standards of righteousness. He was sent to train people to communicate to man what His New Covenant was all about.

f) Disciples – God chose 12 disciples. The 12 disciples were a cross section of all four human temperaments and all of the economic lines and all of the social lines.

g) He spent three years teaching His disciples the standard of God's righteousness.

h) The disciples experienced miracles with Him: casting out demons, bringing the dead back to life, other healings and miracles.

i) The disciples saw Jesus challenge the religious leaders of the day.

j) The disciples watched Jesus weep and laugh with joy.

13. Jesus knew the time of the cross was near. He revealed himself clearly and they now knew with certainty the truth of His mission. Matthew 16:13-28 (Peter's confession).

   d) His disciples needed to be preparing to be disciplers, rather than disciples.

   e) His disciples needed to be teachers, ambassadors, missionaries, and church planters.

   f) Read Matthew 16:13-20 and 23-28.

14. The Holy Spirit – after the death and resurrection of Jesus, The Holy Spirit was breathed on man. Now God lives within us as our constant companion the Holy Spirit which always reminds us of what God wants us to do and what He does not want us to do.

   b) This is neat to me. After Adam and Eve sinned, man could not be in the presence of God or look upon God. God came to earth through His Son Jesus, and then man could see God, feel God and be in the presence of God. God stepped forward one more time and now dwells within man through the Holy Spirit.

15. God's Commission

f) Mark 1:17 "Come and follow me, and I will make you fishers of men."

g) The Great Commission – Mark 28:19-20 "Therefore, go and make disciples of all nations, baptizing them in the name of the Father and the Son and the Holy Spirit, teaching them to obey everything I have commanded you. And surely I am with you always, to the very end of the age."

h) II Corinthians 5:10-11 "For we must all appear before the judgment seat of Christ, that each one may receive what is due him for the thing done while in the body, whether good or bad. Since then, we know what it is to fear the Lord, we try to persuade men."

i) Ephesians 6:18-19 "And pray in the Spirit on all occasions, with all kinds of prayers and requests. With this in mind, be alert and always keep on praying for all the saints."

j) The most compelling verses – Jesus in the Garden of Gethsemane. John 17:13-19; Jesus prays for His disciples. We are now His disciples.

16. Our commission is clear. We are the ambassadors, evangelists, missionaries, teachers, doers, and servants of the Lord. ARE YOU READY FOR THAT? Abraham is dead. Moses is dead. The prophets are dead. You are the living communicator for our living Lord.

c) Ephesians 6:19-20 – I am an ambassador.

d) II Corinthians 5:20 – We are therefore Christ's ambassadors.

MORNING MEDITATION –
A CONVERSATION WITH GOD
10-31-2007

It occurs to me that we, Your creation, have manipulated, twisted, turned and reversed the roles of our creation. Your creation is not about us as individuals, but, rather, we as individuals are about Your creation. We were put here to serve and glorify your name, rather than the opposite. Most of the time, our prayers are focused on asking you to alter our life circumstances to serve our perceived needs and to make our life more comfortable, rather than using those circumstances to serve the purpose and reason for our creation. To put it mildly, our religion has become all about us, rather than all about You. That is dangerous, because "we or I" is the core of all sin. "I" is the center of all sin. Spell the word "sin". What is in the middle of the spelling of the word "sin"? Of course, it is "I". History shows us in the Old Testament how God would bless His people. They would honor Him because of the blessing, but eventually His people would return back to the focus of their concern, which is "I" or "self". When that happened? God would withdrawal His blessing and protection. When God did that, His people would be thrown back into captivity. Question: How long will God tolerate our selfishness and allow us to deny His purpose for our creation? Why is it that we need to be punished before we repent and then return to our calling?

MORNING MEDITATION
7-5-07

As I was sharing some time with you this morning, Lord, I got an old familiar sense of delight when I felt Your presence. I realized that in my prayer time I was talking to You about how to surrender my life to you and how to live with you in harmony each day. Question: How can I surrender my life to you in faith and trust? WOW! What an exciting time! The reason my mind, heart and soul is considering the basis of this type of meditation is because there are many things in my current life situations that are challenging. I do not always fully understand how to deal with these challenging trials at times. During this prayer time and thought process, You revealed to me Your heart's desire. If I could give these trials and challenges to you 100%, then they would no longer be a concern of mine, but simply a concern of Yours. That sounds pretty easy, but is it really that easy? There are always consequences to everything. Then it occurred to me that the consequence of that kind of trust and faith would require obedience to a very important command. That command would require me to be totally content in whatever station of life that I am in and to be content in the circumstances of my life. I would have to be content even unto death. Once again, WOW! Lord, You are sharing with me some of your very intimate secrets.

Then the big question came to my mind. Am I <u>willing</u> to be content in my life situations even if it takes me to total deprivation, to total servant hood and even obedience unto death? Am I willing to trust You to that extent? Well, I guess I had better think that proposition over before I make any impulsive decisions. Once I commit to that, there is no turning back as you revealed in the book of Luke – Luke 12, starting at verse 49. To be called your servant requires a commitment.

"I have come to bring fire on the earth, and how I wish it were already kindled. But I have a baptism to undergo, and how distressed I am until it is completed. Do you think I came to bring peace on earth? No, I tell you, but division. From now on there will be five in one family divided against each other, three against two and two against three. They will be divided, father against son and son against father; mother against daughter and daughter against mother; mother-in-law against daughter-in-law and daughter-in-law against mother-in-law."

Question: What has brought me to this kind of thinking, Lord? You have provided for me so abundantly with safety and comfort in the past by Your grace. Faith and trust was not something that I have really understood. Sure, Lord, I used the terms freely without understanding them. Most of all, I did not understand your version of what faith and trust really is. Now that things have changed in my life's circumstances and I have less control over my life's circumstances, I am starting to understand your version of faith and trust, and I am beginning to realize that so few people really do understand your version of faith and trust.

Here is what is strange and weird: Lord, I really like where you are taking me. I really like this deeper level of intimacy and righteousness that we are sharing together. I feel so close to your heart, to your passion and your mission. I am just starting to identify with the depth of closeness that so many of your chosen people are experiencing. As I study Your Word, the Bible, I have come to realize that You have a passion for the least of these, which includes the poor and less affluent people, and so many of your people are simply surviving minute by minute and day by day.

Lord, You have allowed me to go on many mission trips where I have interacted with thousands of these people who are simply surviving day by day. I am now starting to understand these people with their deep intimacy and sense of righteousness they have with you. I furthermore understand why they consistently say the Americans have no concept of faith and trust, and they rely on their own works and on their own security programs rather than on You. When I go back to the mission field, Lord, I truly believe that I will have a better appreciation for their beautiful prayers and the tears of gratitude that are in their eyes.

After our time of fellowship, I opened the Bible and the Scripture that jumped out at me was Luke 12:4-7. How appropriate that Scripture is to this subject.

JESUS SAID: "I tell you, my friends, do not be afraid of those who kill the body and afterwards can do no more. But I will show you whom you should fear. Fear him who, after killing the body, has power to throw you into hell. Yes, I tell you, fear him. Are not five Sparrows sold for two pennies? Yet not one of them is forgotten by God. Indeed, the very hairs of your head are all numbered. Don't be afraid; you are worth more than many sparrows."

That Scripture sums it up, doesn't it?

MUSLIM TERMINOLOGY & BELIEF SYSTEMS BY TOPIC

Outlined below are some interesting aspects of the belief system advocated by Muhammad through his Koran:

ALLAH - Allah is an Arabic word for "one God". Muhammad proposed that there is only one deified God and that is Allah. Because Christians believe in God, the Father; God the Son; and God, the Holy Spirit, Muhammad labeled Christianity as a polytheistic religion. Muhammad was very clear on this as stated in the Koran, Sura 4:171;5:72-73 and 4:169. Muslims cannot put it together that God, the Father, God the Son and God, the Holy Spirit are one God in three persons.

ISLAM - Islam in its purest form means "peace and submission". Its theoretical meaning is "peace through submission to God". The underlying force driving this is: What are the elements of submission? Does submission mean Jihad (committing murder under the name of "Holy War") or performing all the various acts of ritualism to please Allah and earn a way into a higher place at death? The rule of submission is a very compelling and controlling force. The concept of submission is very dangerous when a man or group of men have the authority to determine the parameters of submission. As an example, an act of submission to Allah is to fly a passenger jet into a heavily populated building for the purpose of killing as many people as possible, just for the sake of killing.

The rewards of submission are interesting. A Muslim man is led to believe that if he dies a martyr's death (as happened on 9-11-01), he will go to a heaven and have forty virgin women at his beckoning. The Koran teachings seem so contradictory. It teaches peace by way of violence.

MUSLIM - Muslim means "to submit to the will of Allah". The Muslims believe that Muhammad was given the revelations of God's will. There are two primary sects of Muslims outside the borders of the United States. On the inside of the United States, there are four sects. The two sects outside the United States' borders are "Shia" and "Sunni". The "Shia" has incorporated some reformed views advocated by Ali – Muhammad's son-in-law. The "Shia" lives mostly in Iran and Iraq. The "Sunni" are scattered through the rest of the Muslim world.

JESUS - How do the fundamental Muslims view Jesus? There are varying accounts, but it is interesting that most accounts consider Him to be a prophet. Muhammad believed Jesus was divinely inspired through the Immaculate Conception but denies His deity. Muslim teaching does not deny the history of Jesus. The Islam religion claims that He was able to perform miracles as a prophet. Muslims believe that the miracles were performed under the power of a prophet but not as the Son of God. Question? Where did Muhammad think that power came from? Where do Muslims today think that power came from? The power to perform miracles could only have come God or from Satan. Jesus used His power to do good for others. Satan does not do good, so the power must have come from God.

There is another interesting point in their teaching concerning Jesus. They deny all of the prophecies before Jesus' birth which were 100% accurate and which foretold Jesus as the awaited Messiah and Deliverer. Muslims deny Jesus' claim to be the Son of God. Because they deny Jesus, they therefore deny the Holy Spirit. THIS IS PURE IGNORANCE ON THEIR PART. They say they believe in the same God as Jews and Christians believe in – the God who created all things – and they acknowledge the prophets and then deny all of the prophecies that foretold the coming of Jesus. Here is the part that is hard for me to understand: If they deny Jesus, then how can they justify a self-proclaimed prophet who has no prophetic history? Muhammad had no prophetic history.

Look at the lives of each – Jesus and Muhammad. Muhammad failed in many things with his biggest failure being that he died and remained dead. Jesus died only to live again in total Glory. History records that Jesus walked again among the people after His crucifixion and death. Muhammad has returned to dust.

We Christians have a tremendous responsibility to educate the Muslim people. If they were given an educated choice, I believe many would choose to follow Jesus.

MUSLIMS AND THE HEREAFTER - Muslims believe that Allah set up a system of accountability. They believe there are a heaven and a hell with admission criteria for both places. The works that are done on earth fall into one of the two criteria as credits or debits. Also, their faithfulness to the rituals is part of the criteria. Once again, the dangers of this type of theology is in determining who defines which works are necessary and to what extent have enough works been done to satisfy the one who defines the works that are necessary. A wicked man can set up some pretty nasty standards for works criteria. We are seeing that being played out right now on a worldwide basis.

JIHAD – Jihad means "a striving in the cause of God". There are various aspects of Jihad, and the highest level of Jihad is to "stand up to a tyrant (an infidel) and to take arms in defense of Islam". The "defense", or type of defense, is declared by the ruling power of religious leadership. Have you ever heard of the old saying, "the best defense is a good offense"? Evidently, Muhammad must have had that in mind when he wrote the Koran. To paraphrase the Koran (Sura 5:51,81;9:4,4,74), it is right to kill the infidel, to make war with the unbelievers and to slay the idolaters. This is only a sampling of many writings in the Koran which justify selective murder.

Guess who is considered to be the primary infidels? You've got it! – The Jews and Christians. Remember that the authority of the ruling religious leadership of the moment defines the method of war. This is dangerous stuff. It is dangerous for this reason: when any religion (in this case, Islam) allows any man to have supreme power and authority to interpret God's word and His will, eventually that man's will, desires and ambitions will take control. A point in case is Osama Bin Laden and the Taliban.

SHARIA - Sharia is the comprehensive Muslim law. The Koran (Quran) and the ruling authority of the religious leadership of the moment derive the law. It governs their moral basis, the basis of beliefs, their ritualistic procedures and even their aspects of daily living, as well as collective living. This is justified as a protection mechanism.

NOTE: This is not the extent of the rituals, customs and beliefs of Islam. There are many more.

MY MORNING DEVOTIONAL TIME
5-30-07

I began thinking about how big God really must be and how powerful He must be. I began thinking about the fact that at one time, this world did not exist as we know it. For that matter, the Universe did not exist. God had the power to create the universe and He had the power to create our world. Everything that I can see or even hear or even think of, He had the power to simply speak that into place. Oh, what a powerful God! Then, I began to think, why would a God with that much power, be interested in somebody as lowly as I am? Why would He care if I even existed?

My thoughts then drifted back to something very basic and something very simple. I think that God created man simply because he wanted to have a friend. I'm not smart enough to know whether God can be a lonely God or not, but I do know that He created man with the intention of having a friend. He created Adam and then he created Eve, and the scripture says He walked with them in the cool of the evening. The implication is that he was happy with His friends. I think He wanted Adam and Eve to be His friends. I think today God is really looking for a friend - one that will make a commitment to be a friend - one that would reverence Him as much as He has, in His own way, reverenced us. He did not have to create us, but He did. We owe absolutely everything to Him. I think He wants a friend - a friend that would love Him back with great intensity - a friend that will walk in the cool of the evening with a commitment to His righteousness. That's pretty basic and pretty simple, but yet that's what I believe God really wants and has allowed me to look into His heart.

That's the thought process that I had this morning in my time of meditation. It is thrilling to feel His closeness and intimacy.

MY VISION OF GOD

After my special time of prayer with my God and my God Savior, Jesus, I sat back and tried to imagine what God looks like. I can get glimpses of His appearance from the book of Revelation, but those descriptions are difficult for me to project an image of. Those descriptions are also descriptions of our God as He administers justice to each cultural situation according to their obedience and lack of obedience. Our God is a sovereign God of total control for discipline, grace and mercy.

Now, back to my imagination of what God looks like. My mind envisions a huge figure so radiant that it is somewhat hard to look at; yet, the beauty is so vibrant that I am compelled to gaze upon Him. I see radiating from Him beams or rays of authority, and yet there is an overwhelming feeling of love, compassion and mercy. As I look upon Him, I am filled with joy and peace. This vision of God causes me to think of my body as it is today - full of pains, weakness, and insignificance. My new body will be perfect, radiant and without pain. My new body will be pain free and full of joy and peace. Oh, what a glorious day that will be!

I hope my imagination will someday be fulfilled when I will sit at the feet of my God and Jesus.

Have you ever tried to think of a heavenly experience? Try it, you may like it.

OUR CALLING AND OUR FOOTPRINTS

In our beginning, our birth, God breathed life into a perfectly formed hand-full of dust. When He breathed life into that hand-full of dust, He also breathed an eternally living spirit and then gave the body a spirit and a commission, or purpose, to serve Him. Everybody is created for a purpose, commonly said to be a "calling". What is yours?

I think I know my calling – When I gave my life to Jesus, it was a transformation to one of the many revelations He gave to me – He gave me a calling for the souls of the lost and to minister to what society calls "the least of these". I felt a calling to the mission field, which at that time I thought was to go to impoverished places and countries. Later, I discovered that my calling and mission field was here with my own family and community. I never lost a desire and an overwhelming need to go to all parts of the world to fulfill the great commission. I can feel the pain of hunger and agony of the down trodden. I can hear the cries of those who are in hell because they did not receive the saving grace of the blood of Jesus. Because of this passion in my heart for "the least of these" and the "lost souls", I have committed my life to what I feel my calling is.

When I gave my life to Christ, I had no idea He would take me down the path that he has. It has been an exciting journey. He has allowed me to minister to victims here in the U.S.A., like victims of hurricane Katrina, victims of a tornado in Smithville, Ms, and especially people of the community I live in. He has also allowed, or called, me to represent him in many countries, like England (3 times), Wales, Germany (3 times), Switzerland, Liechtenstein, France (3 times), Austria, Italy (3 times), Greece, Bulgaria, Venice, Crete, Israel (3 times), Turkey, Jordan (2 times) Syria, South Korea, Japan, The Philippines (11 times), Buenos Aires, Argentina, Mexico (many times), United Arab Emeritus(2 times), Honduras (5 times), Belize, Nepal, Ecuador, Canada (many times), India, Cuba (2) , Bahamas (2 times), South Africa, Malawi Africa, Mozambique Africa, Spain, China and other countries.

Question: Why am I keeping track of this history? Well, everybody leaves footprints in the sands of their life. Hopefully, my footprints are pleasing to God, even though there are footprints that I regret and am ashamed of. God loves you and can use your footprints!

My mission model is Luke 4:18,19:

"The Spirit of the Lord is on me, because he has anointed me to preach good news to the poor. He has sent me to proclaim freedom for the prisoners and recovery of sight for the blind, to release the oppressed, to proclaim the year of the Lord's favor".

My prayer is Ephesians 6:19:

"Pray also for me, that whenever I open my mouth, words may be given me so that I will fearlessly make known the mystery of the gospel, for which I am an ambassador in chains. Pray that I may declare it fearlessly, as I should".

My life's goal and motto - Psalm 119:33-37:

"Teach me, O Lord, to follow your decrees; then I will keep them to the end. Give me understanding, and I will keep your law and obey it with all my heart. Direct me in the path of your commands, for there I find delight. Turn my heart toward your statutes and not toward selfish gain. Turn my eyes away from worthless things; preserve my life according to your word".

My commission – Ephesians 3:8-11

"Although I am less than the least of all God's people, this grace was given to me; to preach to the Gentiles the unsearchable riches of Christ and to make plain to everyone the administration of this mystery, which for ages past was kept hidden in God, who created all things. His intent was that now, through the church, the manifold wisdom of God should be made known to the rulers and authorities in the heavenly realms, according to his eternal purpose which he accomplished in Christ Jesus our Lord."

PEACE AND SATISFACTION

Peace and satisfaction comes from liking what you have instead of always having what you like. Can't always have what you like but you can always like what you have.

POWER

We, as Christians, have a great power. Actually, it may be the greatest power we will ever have. We have the power to show mercy, compassion and love. The use of that power has eternal rewards and, I believe, pleases Jesus to the point that He smiles and says, "Yes, Yes. My followers are doing what I taught". Use your power to ITS FULLEST EXTENT.

SALVATION – WHAT DOES THAT MEAN?

Life is a continuation of experiences that range from good to not so good. Said another way – the "life experience" is always changing. Recently (10/15/09), I had a new experience. To say the least, it was a painfully new experience. On that day I had surgery on my right shoulder. The doctor removed bone spurs from the bone in my shoulder and repaired an extremely long tear in my rotator cuff. After seven days, I could still barely tolerate the pain. Pain pills did not even daunt the pain. The pain was relentless. It was there 24 hours, day and night. I had been spending the night hours without much sleep, sitting upright in a chair to help control the severity of the pain. Hopefully, there would be a day that I could say it was worth it.

I asked the Lord how I could turn this new experience of pain into something positive. What could I learn from this, and how could I grow from this experience? THEN IT CAME TO ME. Pastor Danny Riley once said, "We cannot understand the value of our salvation until we understand the cost of our salvation". I could learn something from this pain and also gain a greater appreciation for my salvation. My pain was confined to my right shoulder and I could barely stand it. Jesus knew in the Garden of Gethsemane what His pain would be. He knew that He would be whipped, beaten, and humiliated. He knew that His flesh would be torn from His body. He knew that He would be nailed to the cross. He knew that He was sinless and yet He would take on all sins of the past, present and future. He knew of pain that we do not know about. He knew all of this. He knew it and after agonizing to the point of death and even sweating drops of blood, He said to the Father, "Not my will but Yours be done". He willingly agreed to take on the PRICE OF PAIN to provide His blood to cover our sin debt. How can I begin to say thank you, Jesus, for what you chose to do because of your love for us?

Did the pain persist for months? Yes. But it is worth it to be a little closer to Jesus. This pain and understanding the pain that Jesus took on adds value to an appreciation for the cost of my salvation. Thank you Jesus!!!

<u>SUCCESS</u>

Success can be tricky to define or, for that matter, to attain. The definition of success can change for an individual with time and circumstances. That is illustrated below.

<u>Time</u> - Think about what you consider successful at age 16 and how does it compare to what you consider successful today.

<u>Circumstance</u> - If you had more to eat than you needed to eat and you found more to eat, would that be a success? - Probably not. How about if you had little to nothing to eat and you found something to eat? Would that be a success? - Probably.

Success can send you into a form of captivity that most people are not aware of. The business world requires us to create and develop a field of specialization that eventually entraps them. Instead of the job opening the door to freedom, it becomes the mechanism of the very thing that requires your attention, time, and consciousness, which actually steals and employs your freedom. The ironic thing about success through specialization is this—the more you specialize, the more you know more and more about less and less.

The measurement of success is always set against a standard. That standard is made up of essentially two forms. The moral code of ethics, which is fairly rigid, and the evolutionary set of standards, which is constantly changing, are based on new information and an attempt to find balance of values as you live and participate in the systems involved in your life's circumstances.

Rigid Code of Ethics - This is a core value set of ethics that usually drives all other values. It could be and should be a belief system that   you believe was constituted by a divine supreme power. It could also be an overwhelming strong power to succeed in an earthly system, like the pursuit of money, power, etc. Evolutionary Ethics - These ethics are usually short term and desire-driven. Example: Is short hair or long hair okay? Are short skirts or long skirts okay? Are tongue rings okay or not?

People have a compelling and overwhelming desire to conform to their environment, especially to social and economic group. I suppose this need draws back upon a herding or clustering instinct for safety and comfort reasons. There is safety in numbers of a like kind.

Without getting into an ethics moral debate or a desires moral debate, I would like to propose a question that was given to me. Is it a blessing or a curse to succeed at something that does not matter? That impacted me for this reason. God put me here to serve a purpose and I only have so much time to fulfill that purpose. When I stand before the Lord, the question that might come is this—What were you successful at that really mattered?

Success to some people is to blend into the cultural system. Eventually people usually gravitate to a system that encompasses their rigid code of ethics and their desired code of ethics. They will blend in and usually be subject to the approval of those people within that system. They spend a lifetime trying to stay in the balance of that system. They want people to approve of them. Being under the judgment of that approval is condemning, until they learn that most people within that group are neither for them or against them, but rather are concerned and thinking only of the betterment for themselves. That is not true of all people, but is true for most people. The real comfort comes when you understand that and your expectations are adjusted accordingly.

What is the method and the answer to success? The answer to that depends. Psychologists would tell you, it depends on when you think you are and what you think you are. Then determining who you want to be and what you want to be. That is what psychology says. I say there is a better way and, in fact, the only way – God's way!

SUCCESS AT WHAT REALLY MATTERS

Without getting into an ethics moral debate or a contentious moral debate, I would like to propose a question that was given to me. Is it a blessing or a curse to succeed at something that does not matter? That is a dynamic question and it impacted me for this reason. After careful thought, my conclusion took me back to the only source of absolute truth which is as follows. God put me here to serve a purpose – His purpose, not a self-absorbed, self-elevated purpose. I only have so much time and energy to fulfill that purpose. The significance of that question is huge because when I stand before the Lord, the question that might come is this; you had success with your time on earth but was your success all about you, or did your success have eternal value? If your success was about you, it does not matter.

Success to some people is tied to the cultural system or a self-contrived, self-serving system. These people usually gravitate to a system that encompasses their desired code of ethics and also endorses their own vain desires. They will blend in and usually be subject to the approval of those people within that similar system. They spend a lifetime attempting to clone each other in the system and to stay within the balance of the system. They want people to approve of them so that their self-gratifying desires can be met. Being under the judgment of seeking the approval of that system is self-consuming until they learn that most people within that system are not for or against them, but rather, are concerned and thinking only of the betterment of themselves. It is hopeless to find any level of long term peace and contentment when a person seeks to serve self. That is not true of all people, but is true for most people. The real comfort and freedom comes when you understand the people of that system or culture could care very little about you and are focused on being served by the system rather than to serve you or the system. When you realize that fact, you should not be surprised when you as a person have no value to anybody in the system or to the system itself.

What are the methods and the answer to succeeding at what matters? The answer to that question depends on your frame of reference. Psychiatrists and psychologists would tell you that self-perception is everything. Their answer to joy and to the question of what really matters is tied to meeting your desires and to be served rather than to serve. The bible says something different. The bible says we were created for a special purpose. God created each one of us to be unique. He did not want us to be lost in some kind of a social system or a self- derived cultural system. It is hopeless to find any level of long term peace and contentment apart from the creator's plan. I say that there is a better way, and in fact, the only way – God's way!

The purpose for you and the fulfillment of that purpose is where you will find real success in what really matters. The bible was given in such a way that you can find your purpose and a real value in what really matters, if you study His word, seek to serve him and to develop an intimate relationship with

Jesus that will ultimately lead to "what really matters" and ultimate joy.

SUCCESS IS NOT EASY

Success is like fighting a war. You cannot quit when you get tired. Success is just like that. Success comes when you persevere after the enemy (the elements that resist success) gets tired. Never give up – Never give up – Never give up.

<u>THE HEART</u>
"Man looks at the outward actions of a person, but God looks at the heart." - I Samuel 16:7

I attended a Wednesday night Bible teaching led by David Ball at Anchor Church. As usual, he preached a powerful message about how God views us. God looks at our hearts and also forgives our sinful actions. Most people control their actions, or give the perception of controlling the actions of their sinful nature. While they do not show their sins among other people, their hearts are filled with lust, greed, anger, hate and self-serving desires. Sure, God does not like the actions of sin but is most concerned by what is on the inside – our heart for him. He wants us to have a passionate desire and heart to love and serve Him.

We can fool each other about the perceptions we present to each other, but we cannot fool God. He looks at the heart. I am so thankful for that!!! There are times that I sin and do not know it, and there are other times I sin and know it while I am doing it. Afterward, I ask myself "How stupid can I get? I am sorry." But, thank you God for looking at my heart. I can truly say that I passionately love you and I am a man after your heart. I want to serve you, Lord. This is my only hope.

King David is a perfect example of how God views us. David was a sinful man. He lusted after another man's wife and then had her husband killed. David had many terrible acts of disobedience, but God loved David. God loved David because he was a man after the heart of God. David sincerely loved God even though he was stupid about the way he lived his life. Because of David's love for God, God loved him even as a friend. Lord please give me the same love for You as David had! I want to have Your love. I want to be Your friend! I want to serve You!

I am so thankful that God judges my heart and not just my actions.

THE LOVE OF JESUS IS FOR YOU

Love is a powerful force and does create dynamic consequences. There appears to be a desire for love in all of God's creation where emotion is present. Among all animals, the greatest desire for love is shown by human beings. The need for love is so powerful that a person's character is shaped by the amount of love or the lack of love that the person has received. Love, as essential as it is, can be fickle. Fickle in this respect – it is far too often given conditionally. Conditional love can carry serious emotional consequences.

IS THERE SUCH A THING AS UNCONDITIONAL LOVE? IF THERE IS, HOW CAN I FIND IT? Answer – at the time of creation, God made a provision <u>Jesus, was sacrificed by God Himself</u> to provide the blood to cover our sins so that we could be presented <u>pure</u> and <u>holy</u> before Him, our God. The blood of Jesus was offered to cover our sins. For God to offer the blood of Jesus, Jesus had to die. The way God chose the death of Jesus was not an easy and painless death. God allowed all of the sin and hatred that Satan has in store for those who choose the way of the world to be unleashed onto Jesus. His death was a brutal death unlike any other man could offer. What God did at the cross with Jesus was an irrevocable covenant between man and God, demonstrating unconditional love. Once you surrender your life to Jesus, the irrevocable, unconditional contract is in place for eternity. God loves you and He showed that love at the cross.

The Love of Jesus – Jesus demonstrated His love for you and all of us by choosing to go to the cross for us. Jesus foreknew the pain and suffering He would go through at the cross. He foreknew the pain of every piece of flesh that would be torn from His body. He foreknew the hurt of the whips and the rods that would pulverize His flesh. He foreknew the agony of the cross before it happened. He foreknew the personal hurt and the anguish of being temporarily separated from His Father. I know He foreknew it because He anguished close to death in the Garden of Gethsemane (Matthew 26 vs. 38).

"Then He said to them, 'My soul is overwhelmed with sorrow to the point of death. Stay here and keep watch with me.'"

I know He foreknew it because he anguished to the point of sweating drops of blood. (Luke 22 vs. 44) -

"And being in anguish, he prayed more earnestly, and his sweat was like drops of blood falling to the ground."

Yet, though He had the option to not go to the Cross, He chose to do it to demonstrate His love for you. Wow. What can I say? What can I do but to worship Him? He sacrificed His life for you and me and all of mankind. Love, the love of Jesus, is a powerful force that will have a dynamic force in your life. Let this love of Jesus come into your life and see what will happen.

THE MEANING OF THE "STAR SPANGLED BANNER"

At various events where the "Star Spangled Banner" is sung, I wonder if those who are singing the words know what they are singing. Just for a minute, let's consider the history and depth of the meaning of the words.

During the British and Colonial war in 1814, the British had successfully captured and burned the city of Washington. The British had put together an overwhelming naval force to discourage and defeat the colonists. They amassed over 200 war ships and sailed up the port at the Baltimore Harbor in Maryland to Fort McHenry. The British had captured many colonial soldiers and the soldiers were held on some war ships. The Colonial Army had captured many British soldiers as well. There was a large colonial resistance at Fort McHenry. Frances Scott Key went on board the British Command ship to negotiate a trade of prisoners and for a special person named Dr. William Beanes. Unbeknown to Frances Scott Key, the commander of the British Fleet sent a message to the Commander of the forces at Fort McHenry to surrender or the fort and its soldiers would be bombed to the point of annihilation. To signify their surrender and avoid the attack, the Colonial Army was required to remove the American Flag that was flying high over the fort. They did not remove the flag, but actually waved it more vigorously, which meant they would not surrender.

The British started bombing the fort with thousands upon thousands of bombs from their warships. The bombings started in the afternoon and lasted all night into the next day. The bombs demolished the fort and had many, many direct hits on the flag. The British wondered how that flag could still be standing. What was discovered is this: When the flag took a direct hit and knocked it down, the soldiers would go over and reset the flag because they would not surrender. The soldiers reset the flag many, many times during the ordeal. When it was over, they found over 100 dead bodies of soldiers who protected and reset the flag. (Note: The price of our freedom has come at a large price of true American Patriots. They gave their lives and their fortunes. I thank them from the bottom of my heart).

While the bombing was going on, Frances Scott Key was on the Commander of the British Navy's ship. The colonial prisoners were also on board the ship. Frances Scott Key was keeping the prisoners informed of the battle. From this experience, Frances Scott Key wrote the words for the "Star Spangled

Banner". This was a tribute for the love that these prisoners and the other colonists had for America and its flag.

Please understand these words of the "Star Spangled Banner" are rich in loyalty, commitment, sacrifice and a sincere love for the basics that this country was founded on. The greatest foundation block that this country was founded on was only four words – IN GOD WE TRUST. I wonder what the founders would think if they knew what was going on in America today.

STAR SPANGLED BANNER
Oh, say can you see by the dawn's early light
What so proudly we hailed at the twilight's last gleaming?
Whose broad stripes and bright stars, through the perilous fight,
O'er the ramparts we watched were so gallantly streaming.
And the rocket's red glare, the bombs bursting in air,
Gave proof through the night that our flag was still there.
O, say does that star-spangled banner yet wave
O'er the land of the free and the home of the brave?

Analysis of the Words:
vt.
After a whole night of bombing, the prisoners were asking with great anticipation, "Is the flag still standing" because they did not want to surrender.

What so proudly we hailed at the twilight's last gleaming.

The flag was proudly flying before it turned dark. I can only imagine they spent the whole night cheering on their fellow patriots.

Whose broad stripes and bright stars, through the perilous flight, o'er the ramparts we watched were so gallantly streaming. And the rocket's red glare, the bombs bursting in air, gave proof through the night that our flag was still there.

These verses describe the battle that took place over the night and their joy to see the flag was still standing. That flag and what it stood for meant so much to them. It meant so much to them that they were willing to die for it.

Oh, say does that star-spangled banner yet wave, o'er the land of the free and the home of the brave?

This verse describes their total joy of the fact that they paid the price of victory. They wanted a land that was free and they wanted a home for the brave.

I hope that the next time that you sing the "Star Spangled Banner" or hear it being sung, it will have an extra special meaning and maybe have a respect and gratitude for the cost of your freedom.

Question: I wonder if the illegal immigrants will ever have any respect or gratitude for the freedom and quality of life they are experiencing here in the USA. How much blood, sweat and tears did their ancestors give for the land of the free and the home of the brave?

Question: I wonder if the liberal American citizens know about, or even care about, the cost of acquiring, and the cost of maintaining the freedoms, comfort and safety we so richly enjoy.

THE MOUTH

The mouth—what a wonderful and important thing it can be. It allows you to enjoy some of the blessings of Our Lord. Some of the most joyful times is when we are using our mouths to eat. The mouth can also be a vital tool used to express and communicate through verbalization. The mouth, while it can be a nice thing, can also be a vicious tool or a weapon that can be used for pure destruction. More wars, destruction, and hurt have been brought about by words that come from the mouth, than any other mechanism.

Words can be a tool of destruction, but, words can also be a thing of beauty. What better mechanism for communication do we have than words coming from the mouth? Also, what feels better than a kind word that comes from the mouth?

The Bible has hundreds of references to the mouth in both the New and the Old Testament. The Bible records a lot of cases where the mouth was a tool or a weapon. The Bible also records many cases, the mouth gave words of comfort and joy and reassurances. In the New Testament, Jesus gave a statement about words used in the wrong way, Matthew 15:10. The mouth in this scripture, is referred to as a weapon because of the words that come out of it. Refer to Matthew 15: vs.10-20. Verse 10 says it very clearly:

> Matthew 15: vs.10 - Jesus called the crowd to Him and said, "Listen and understand. What goes into a man's mouth does not make him 'unclean', but what comes out of his mouth, that is what makes him 'unclean'.

The rest of those verses, verses 10-20, go on to clarify what He is referring to.

Words, we all use them. Jesus said to be careful that your words are cleansing and be sure your words are clean, not unclean. This whole dissertation is about this: the essence, character, and soul of a man is not so much about what a man puts into his body from the outside in, but rather the essence, character and soul of a man is reflected by what comes from the inside out through his words, deeds, and actions.

THE PASSION OF JESUS CHRIST
AND HIS PRAYERS

The Passion of Jesus Christ can easily be summed up as follows. Jesus' Passion is that he came to reveal the nature of his Holy Father. The question is this: How did this Passion manifest itself towards all of his creation and specifically towards man?

What was and what are the various aspects of the Passion of Christ? To understand the aspects of His Passion, I must first define Passion. Passion is that property, emotion, and zeal that is the very core of the driving force that defines and describes who we are, what we represent, and what represents the calling of our creation.

If we are called to be like Jesus, then we must know His Passion. If we know His Passions, then we can know what our Passions are supposed to be. These passions showed up in the prayers of Jesus. Hopefully, this brief review of the prayers of Jesus may enable us to have a glimpse of a small part of the Passion of Jesus. Knowing the prayers of Jesus allows us to peek at the very heart of Jesus. Prayer was the most intimate relationship Jesus had with His Father. Our prayers should be the same.

THE STANDARD

The standard of the church and that of a Christian was given by Paul in his letter to every "Christian in the city of Philippi."

"Is there any such thing as Christians cheering each other up? Do you love me enough to want to help me? Does it mean anything to you that we are brothers in the Lord, sharing the same Spirit? Are your hearts tender and sympathetic at all? Then make me truly happy by loving each other and agreeing wholeheartedly with each other, working together with one heart and mind and purpose.

Don't be selfish; don't live to make a good impression on others. Be humble, thinking of others as better than yourself. Don't just think about your own affairs, but be interested in others, too, and in what they are doing.

Your attitude should be the kind that was shown us by Jesus Christ, who, though He was God, did not demand and cling to his rights as God, but laid aside his mighty power and glory, taking the disguise of a slave and becoming like men. And he humbled himself even further, going so far as actually to die a criminal's death on a cross." Philippians 2:1-8 (The Living Bible)

THE TRANSFIGURATION

Matthew 17, vs. 1-13. These verses have to be totally inspiring. Peter, James, and John make an entry into the record book of history. They made a written record of what happened when they saw the Transfiguration.

"After six days Jesus took with him Peter, James and John the brother of James, and led them up a high mountain by themselves. There he was transfigured before them. His face shown like the sun, and his clothes became as white as the light. Just then there appeared before them Moses and Elijah, talking with Jesus.

Peter said to Jesus, "Lord, it is good for us to be here. If you wish, I will put up three shelters—one for you, one for Moses and one for Elijah." While he was still speaking, a bright cloud enveloped them, and a voice from the cloud said, "This is my Son, whom I love; with him I am well pleased. Listen to him!"

When the disciples heard this, they fell face-down to the ground, terrified. But Jesus came and touched them. "Get up," he said. "Don't be afraid." When they looked up, they saw no one except Jesus.

As they were coming down the mountain, Jesus instructed them, "Don't tell anyone what you have seen, until the Son of Man Has been raised from the dead." The disciples asked him, "Why then do teachers of the law say that Elijah must come first?"

Jesus replied, "To be sure, Elijah comes and will restore all things. But I tell you, Elijah has already come, and they did not recognize him, but have done to him everything they wished. In the same way the Son of Man is going to suffer at their hands." Then the disciples understood that he was talking to them about John the Baptist.

Isn't that amazing? It is a matter of recorded history that Jesus met with Moses and Elijah. Both Moses and Elijah had already been declared dead by man.

It would appear to be completely out of the realm of possibility that Jesus would have even known Moses and Elijah, except that Jesus was with God before the creation of the earth. Jesus was part of Moses' and Elijah's ministry before it began. Jesus knew them even before their creation. You can check that out in John 17: vs. 5.

"And now, Father, glorify me in your presence with the glory I had with you before the world began".

THOUGHTS ON EVOLUTION OF A SPECIES

Thoughts – why do I have them? I do not know. I just do. Well, yesterday I was holding my dog. As she was sitting on my lap, I was petting her hair. Then it occurred to me about how many hairs were on her body. If the hairs could be counted, the number would exceed our human numbering system by over a power of 10 expressed as an expediential.

Here is the thought: Every fiber in our body, every molecule in our body, every temperament trait of our mind, every hair on our body is described by a DNA code. As an example, the hair that is on my dog's body has a DNA code that determines its placement, its duration, its color, its length, etc. That is a lot of control that the DNA has for one hair. For all of the other hairs, there is a DNA code that describes them too. By the way, that is just one hair. What about the rest of the dog's body, like the eyes, ears, nervous system, etc? Every cell in our body has a DNA code. Unbelievable! Question: In what way can evolution ever account for something this complex? Oh, by the way, my dog is only one species of a genus. What about all the other genus's with their species? Do you want to hear a joke? Here it is – Evolution of the genus and the species. Ha, ha, ha.

What about the reproduction process where the egg and the sperm unite? I had to take courses in college to study biology. Part of those courses was a study of genetics. The thing that fascinated me most in these studies was the egg and the sperm. The size of the egg that created my dog was probably the size of the ball in a ball point pen, and the size of the sperm was probably 100 times smaller than the egg. Yet, as small as they were, the DNA coding, as complex as it is, of the female and male were inscribed in the egg and sperm. Think of all the information that was incorporated and coded into that tiny little egg and the sperm to create a new and unique dog.

Note: a point to be made – Is evolution possible. Yes. Actually, it is a fact. The body is always evolving within its own species through cell division. As our body changes, it is mutating and evolving. As an example, our bodies are always changing. We get bigger and smaller and are always aging, etc.

Now, with regard to the evolution of a new species – It is impossible to combine the egg of a cat with the sperm of a dog to create a new species. Science can scientifically prove that. The study of genetics was fun. Boy, isn't our God a mighty God to have created all of these interdependent systems that work so well together?

Here come my thoughts again. There are some who say they believe my dog, with all of this complexity, is a product of evolution. Hello? Get real! The evolution of my dog as a species is not possible. Now, is it possible that those people believe they are a product of evolution of their own species? Well, if they believe that, then maybe their mother was a monkey! They may be right, at least in their own minds. Their intellect and beliefs would lead me to believe they might be correct if their evolution was possible. Maybe their mother was a monkey. Let that be as it may. I believe what God said is true as stated in the Bible. The Bible says that God created Adam and Eve and we are descendents of Adam and Eve.

Conclusion regarding evolution – Yes, there is evolution within a species. No, there is not evolution of a species. This can be proven scientifically.

Oh, by the way, there is one more of God's word that is something to consider.

"Stop fooling yourselves. If you can count yourself above average in intelligence, as judged by the world's standards, you had better put this all aside and be a fool rather than let it hold you back from the true wisdom from above. For the wisdom of this world is foolishness to God. As it says in the book of Job, God uses man's own brilliance to trap him; he stumbles over his own "wisdom" and falls.

And again, in the book of Psalms, we are told that the Lord knows full and well how the human mind reasons, and how foolish and futile it is -"1 Corinthians 3:18-20.

Please consider these thoughts as Something to Consider.

WALKING WITH THE LORD
(October 23, 2012)

My daily routine is to start my morning with a two-mile walk at 5:30 a.m. on a road at a state park that has lots of trees. This morning the sky was so clear and filled with stars everywhere. The beauty of the stars was indescribable. It occurred to me that the sky was only beautiful because a person was there to observe it. It was beautiful to me. Then it occurred to me that everything I was seeing would be pointless and have no value unless there was a God who created it. To summarize it: If there were no God and no people, the stars in the sky and the universe would have no value or purpose. Actually, the universe would not exist without value and purpose. My conclusion falls back on the dynamics of physics and chemistry, and I realize that everything in the universe is a part of some form of harmonic balance that would be extremely difficult to achieve without divine intervention.

All of this can be summed up by realizing that all of the universe and humanity fell into place because God created it to be just like it is. WOW! I feel so privileged to see the beauty of God's creation and to realize that all the beautiful stars in the sky could not exist without a creator. Wow! Thank you God for letting me have the eyes to see your beauty, the mind to understand your beauty, and the spirit within me to realize that all of the beauty of the night and your universe came from you. WOW!

I love the fellowship I have each morning as I walk with the Lord. What a beautiful experience!

WE ARE DIRT

Are we only a handful of dust, which is dirt? As unflattering as that sounds, we are only dirt. Well, maybe a special kind of dirt. We are made from the elements of the ground, suspended in a molecular state, held together by gases, such as oxygen and hydrogen, which are also in a molecular state, formed by the magnetic fields of atoms, which they, themselves, are a magnetic field. What a miracle! To prove that is true, consider cremation of an animal. A two-hundred pound animal that is cremated will be reduced to a handful of dust, which is dirt. The rest of the body returns to gases. Wait a minute! There is something even more special than the dirt that we are made of - a soul. A soul was also created, along with the dirt. So, the soul and dirt act as one unit. Here is another thought - the most awesome aspect of a created human being is that man's body was made from existing dirt that God formed and breathed life into, and someday the body will return to dirt. But, the soul that was created to occupy the body was created by a spirit that did not exist prior to the creation of the body. While the dirt will return to dirt, the spirit comes from nothing that has physical properties and will never die.

> "The time came when the Lord God formed a man's body from the dust of the ground and breathed into it the breath of life. And man became a living person." - Genesis 2:7

> "All your life you will sweat to master it (the soil), until your dying day. Then you will return to the ground from which you came. For you were made from the ground, and to the ground you will return."- Genesis 3:19

Okay, so what is the point of what has been discussed? Well, no matter how important we think we are, no matter how rich or poor we are, no matter how much civil power we have, no matter about anything else, we were made from dirt; we are now dirt, and we will return to dirt. The bible refers to it as "dust", which is dirt. The thing that separates one special piece of dirt from another special piece of dirt is the unique spirit that occupies each special peace of dirt. The dirt will return to dirt, but the spirit lives on forever in either the agony of hell or the glory of heaven. Do you know Jesus as your Savior so that your eternal spirit can live in heaven, or will your eternal spirit burn in hell?

Just as a note from one piece of dirt to another piece of dirt. Do not evaluate yourself over someone else. They may be a piece of dirt, but so are you. God breathed life into your special piece of dirt, so that you can find, joy, peace and fulfillment by serving Him.

"As a father has compassion on his children so the Lord has compassion on those who fear him for he knows how we are formed; he remembers that we are dirt." –Psalm 103:13

Yes, He Loves you – the dirt and the spirit – ALL of you.

WHAT CAN THE KING OF THE FOREST TEACH US?

In the story of The Wizard of Oz, the lion sang, "If I were King of the forest". Well, he was King of a forest. Just like the lion, you are also King of a forest, THE FOREST BEING YOUR ATTITUDES, ACTIONS AND AREA OF INFLUENCE. Just think about that. You are the King of the most important forest in the world – your forest.

Each day marks the beginning of a significant moment in time. That moment started the creation of a new and very important person. That important person is YOU. You have a very important area of influence, and that is—you are responsible for your own forest. You are making an impact on many lives, so be a good ruler over your forest.

Today is a special day to celebrate your day as King of your forest. God gave you this special day so that you would rule over and have control over your forest of attitude, actions, and influences. The question is: How does a ruler – rule? He rules with wisdom, by understanding the controlling factors of his creation. What is the guidebook of these controlling factors? Of course – the Guidebook is the last-known Truth given to man – The Holy Bible.

Have a wonderful day as King over your forest. God loves you enough to make you a King of your own personal forest.

What Makes a Winner?

Man O'War was the greatest race horse that ever lived. In his lifetime he ran only 21 races with a total racing time of 33 minutes, 32 seconds. Think about that. In all his life, Man O'War ran in competition for only one-half hour. And that is what history remembers—<u>only his races in competition.</u>

But the days and weeks and months of stubborn and relentless training, the days and weeks and months with no one in the grandstands, with no one to cheer him on but his own desire and ambition—these were the important things. These were the things that really made him a champion. You see, he was good when he didn't have to be; he was good when no one else was watching. And that, to me, is the true mark of a champion.

Living a Christian life is certainly not like running a horse race; however, some of the principles can be generalized. The toughest, the most grueling competition in life is that which a Godly person sets up for himself when no one is watching. It's doing the job that our Lord wants done and doing it better than it need be done. It's the hours of unnoticed meditation, prayer, and study of His Word. It's that loneliness of a separated life. It's the unrewarded compassion and help offered to the less fortunate. It's simply being Godly when no one else thinks you have to be.

As for the victory—the world may see you as a loser, but the Lord will see a true thoroughbred. The Lord and the angels in heaven will declare you a champion for eternity!

WORRY

Worry can be a slow poison that can kill and rob you of the joy and hope in your life. Worry can blind a person to all the rich blessings that God has placed in your life for your good and enjoyment. Worry can be used by Satan to discourage a person so that a person cannot reach the potential that person was created for.

Worry – It is your choice.

WORSHIP

Worship – the act of religious reverence and homage paid to God. There are a variety of definitions of worship, depending on the application of the word. In a church or religious application, the definition above is probably most accurate when the word is relevant to God.

Praise – Praise is an act of worship, but not the only act of worship. Actually, praise may not be the most reverent act of worship. Praise can take the form of prayer, bodily expression, vocal (like speaking in tongues), or singing and music. Too often, worship begins and ends with these acts and are only occasionally extended to service for the Lord. These acts are good, but they are only a small part of worship. The greatest part of worship is demonstrated by our physical act of love through our service to God. The focus of Jesus' ministry focused on service.

Service to God – "lateuo" – "to serve and render religious service or homage" – is translated "to worship". The RV renders it (meaning worship) to serve. Note: Taken from Vine's dictionary.

Praise was more of an Old Testament command of God. The reason why I believe there was a re-direct of the emphasis on praise is this: When Adam sinned, God had a disconnect with Adam and his descendents. He did not deal with His people directly, but through intercessors like the prophets and Moses and only a select few. God wanted His people to long for Him, so He desired their praises which were His people's best form of worship at that time. Now, through Jesus, He has a new connection to His people in the flesh, similar to the Garden of Eden. Jesus was God in the flesh. Praise – is it needed and good? Yes! I think praise is good, but service to and through His Son Jesus is most desired.

As we read the New Testament, we can notice Jesus discouraged praise by words and encouraged worship by deeds. There are so many illustrations where He rebuked the words, and, actually, I cannot find many places where He asked for praise through words and song. One example about words and praises that comes to mind is Matthew 23 where He rebuked and called the Pharisees hypocrites because their actions did not match their words. Hypocrisy was the act that angered Jesus most. Actually, hypocrisy was always connected to the place of hell. Jesus did not accept their words and songs and praise as a true worship to God. Somebody needs to show me where Jesus asked for praises through words and music as is used in most churches today. The greatest form of worship is demonstrated in Matthew 25 as a sheep, rather than a goat. Actually, read the last verse of Matthew 25. Those who act as a goat are condemned to hell. WOW. It appears that Jesus finds more delight by us using our resources to serve Him by serving others. Jesus came to serve and show us how to serve. Jesus loves His people and especially what humans call "the least of these". Jesus loved them so much, He wept for them. In fact, Jesus said he came for the "least of these".

It is my observation that Jesus was very intense about His mission. My observation is that He came to offer His blood as a sacrifice to forgive our sins. Next to that blood sacrifice, He came to show us how to serve, how to give and how to forgive. Most all of God's standards of righteousness are centered on these three things. If that is true, then to worship Him is to do what He came to show us – how to serve, how to give and how to forgive.

Paul describes worship in Romans 12:1,2:

"Therefore, I urge you, brothers, in view of God's mercy, to offer your bodies as living sacrifices, holy and pleasing to God – which is your spiritual worship. Do not conform any longer to the pattern of this world, but be transformed by the renewing of your mind. Then you will be able to test and approve what God's will is – His good, pleasing and perfect will".

This, to me, describes the greatest form of worship to God. The greatest form of worship is not by the words of our mouth, or the movements of our body, or all of the rituals that are performed, but, rather, our intimate relationship with Him to serve the purpose for which we were created.

Please accept this treatise as something to consider and apply to our lives. I understand that this treatise may not be accepted very well in many instances, so I employ you to do an unbiased study for yourself. My life model is "Read, listen and observe, not to believe and take for granted, nor to refute or contradict, but to weigh and consider". Because of that, I have concluded this report based on the findings of my research.

WORTHY SAYINGS
Collected by Dorinda Leatherman

When trusting God… He takes us one step at a time. We don't need to see the whole path. Sometimes we need to understand that we don't need to understand!
Max Lucado

When I thought nothing was happening, God, in fact, had me in training. From Something to Consider
by David Leatherman

To withstand trials and temptations – stand with Jesus.
Sign outside a church

God is always in control. We never are. We think we are in control when things are going well. Sometimes God allows us to experience upheaval in all areas of our lives to remind us that He is the Blessed Controller.
A friend

No matter what someone has done to you, you can love that person. Jesus said to "love your enemies" and to "pray for those who despitefully use you." Therefore, He will give you the grace and ability to do so when you are willing. The grace to do what Jesus asks is not given before a willingness to obey. This is "tough love".
From A Call to Worship radio program

Only the Holy Spirit can soften someone's heart and cause him to see the pain he has caused someone. That is why a non- believer or a backslidden Christian really does not know what he is doing. (As Jesus said from the cross as He forgave those who crucified Him.)
From Something to Consider
by David Leatherman

I came to the swift, raging river, and the roar held the echo of fear. "Oh, Lord, give me wings to fly over, if You are, as You promised quite near." But, He said, "Trust the grace I am giving all-pervasive sufficient for you. Take my hand, we will face this together. But my plan is – not over – but through."

Lee Webber

Fear is not from God. It is from the enemy. BUT, it does not have to be our enemy. Fear, when we acknowledge it to God, can serve to grow our faith, not weaken it, and make us stronger. Fear will not overwhelm us when we take our fears to Jesus.

D. Kernsey – A Call to Worship

CHAPTER 3 –

MISSION TRIPS

CUBAN MISSION TRIP – 2014

n the month of April, 2014, I had another opportunity to go to Cuba for the second time. We worked out of Havana. It was an amazing trip again. The people of Cuba seemed real nice. They were reserved, but once you got to know them, they were very social and funny. I am always amazed by the freedom of religion in Cuba. A multitude of religious belief systems practice there – Hindu, Buddha, Islam, Catholicism, and even Christianity. Actually, freedom of religion is part of Cuba's governing constitution. I would like to share a couple of testimonials.

1. Maybe three or four days we walked the streets of Havana sharing the gospel openly and freely. The people were not rude or confrontational. Actually, they were curious and receptive.

2. My primary translator's name was Mike. He was leading approximately 40 college students in Christian fellowship meetings three to four days a week. As we shared in our spare time, he said he had a girl friend that had a deep passion for leading people to Christ. He was interested in her but was

intimidated by her because he did not have the same passion. That evening we went out to a beautiful park and asked people if we could talk to them about Jesus. Every person we asked said yes. That evening 12 people prayed to receive Christ. The very first person we talked to was an advocate communist. When he received Christ, he was so happy and said "something has happened to me". The twelfth person was an older lady with her granddaughter. We saw the grandmother and granddaughter talking and went over and asked the grandmother if we could talk to her about Jesus. She appeared to be totally shocked. She said her granddaughter was asking her questions about Jesus and she did not know the answers. We shared with her the Biblical truth about Creation to Salvation. She and her granddaughter asked Jesus into their hearts. The grandmother could not stop crying because of the joy of knowing Jesus. God seems to arrange "coincidences" like this. These "coincidences" happen all the time.

After we finished, I asked Mike if he now understood the passion his girl friend had for lost souls. He was overjoyed because of this experience and he now has a passion for lost souls. Jesus did a work in his life. He said he would take this message to the students he was mentoring. Again, thank you Jesus. Another young man who was a leader of a different small group accepted Jesus and could not stop saying "Something has happened. I have a strange feeling". He was so happy. I believe the strange feeling was when the Holy Spirit entered into him. I feel that the Holy Spirit was in the middle of all of this.

3. Met with other Christians, of which half were college students, on this same beautiful boulevard. A doctor came with a guitar and we sang praise songs to Jesus. Brother was that fun! This group got together every weekend to sing songs on the boulevard in Havana. WOW! What an experience. I felt the presence of God in the middle of this.

4. On the way back, we had an overnight layover in Cancun, I met a man who was a doctor from Canada. We met on the flat rooftop of the hotel. He also accepted Jesus at 11:30 p.m. He was so happy. He also cried and kept hugging me. He said he had never felt like this before. I felt the presence of God right in the middle of this.

Conclusion: Jesus is alive and well on planet earth. He is showing Himself in different and unexpected places. Thank you, Lord, for allowing me to be in the middle of your work.

GREECE TRIP

Greece – At one time Greece was a beautiful and powerful country, but times have changed. Now Greece is a country of Islamic civil war. What a shame! The objective of this trip was to view the remains of its history and to study its culture and to share the saving grace of Jesus Christ when possible. We were able to see the road to Corinth, theater at Dodona, Agora in Athens, all the temples, the Parthenon in Athens, the great Corinth canal that was hand dug between the mainland and the Peloponnesus Peninsula (which was unbelievable), and also the city of Corinth.

Corinth – What a beautiful city in its day, but also a very sinful city. Paul was a mighty warrior for Jesus. He relent-lessly stood strong for the gospel of Jesus. It was a difficult challenge for Paul since Corinth was a totally self-reliant and self-sufficient city. Corinth was the cultural center, financial center, import and export center and the intellectual center of Southern Greece. Everywhere you looked, you could see great statues of men in a thinking posture to represent a place of great intellect and pride. Because of their reliance on knowledge and their self-proclaimed wisdom, they could not see a need for God (kind of like here in the USA). That did not detour Paul. He stood in front of their greatest minds and presented the gospel of Jesus Christ. Many were saved. Paul was a man of God.

We viewed the rock platform that Paul debated from. I am amazed at the courage of Paul. After seeing all of this, I understand Paul's letters to the Corinthians where he admonished them for their reliance on wisdom and knowledge. The book of Corinthians is full of passages about man's reliance on wisdom and knowledge.

> I Corinthians 1:18-25 - "For the message of the cross is foolishness to those who are perishing, but to us who are being saved, it is the power of God. For it is written: 'I will destroy the wisdom of the wise, the intelligence of the intelligent I will frustrate.
>
> "Where is the wise man? Where is the scholar? Where is the philosopher of this age? Has not God made foolish the wisdom of the world? For since, in the wisdom of God, the world through its wisdom did not know him, God was pleased through the foolishness of what was preached to save those who believe. Jews demand miraculous signs and Greeks look for wisdom.
>
> "But we preach Christ crucified, a stumbling block to Jews and foolishness to Gentiles, but to those whom God has called, both Jews and Greeks, Christ, the power of God and the wisdom of God. For the foolishness of God is wiser than man's wisdom, and the weakness of God is stronger than man's strength."
>
> I Corinthians 2:6-10 - "We do, however, speak a message of wisdom among the mature, but

not the wisdom of this age or of the rulers of this age, who are coming to nothing. No, we speak of God's secret wisdom, a wisdom that has been hidden and that God destined for our glory before time began. None of the rulers of this age understood it, for if they had, they would not have crucified the Lord of glory. However, as it is written: 'No eye has seen; no ear has heard; no mind has conceived what God has prepared for those who love him', but God has revealed it to us by his Spirit. The Spirit searches all things, even the deep things of God."

Sin in Corinth – Since the great thinkers defined their own standard of righteousness, they were guided into a sexual perversion of sin. Sexual sin was rampant in the country of Greece and in the city of Corinth. Since Corinth was a port city, the city had a constant flow of businessmen that wanted entertainment. There was a large stage carved out of rock. For the sake of business, the mothers would offer their daughters to be placed on that stage in nakedness. The business men would openly rape and torment these young girls, in some cases, to the point of death, for their entertainment. Some sins have no limit. Of course, there were many other sinful things being done, but this seemed to me to be the most horrid.

The Fish Symbol – We were told that the fish symbol that is used by Christians today was initiated in Corinth by believers in Corinth. The symbol was used by the believers in Corinth to secretly identify each other as believers.

Cultural Traits – Generally speaking, I found the people of Greece to be rude and abrasive. They also had a hatred for Americans, which is understandable since they are mainly Islamic and Arabic descendants of Ishmael. I also noted the people did not smile much or show any sense of joy. Oh well, that is their life choice, and it goes along with the Islamic belief system.

Conclusion: After seeing the massive structures, it is evident that this country was at one time a great and mighty civilization. It is also evident they are no longer great or mighty as a country or civilization. The next observation was regarding Paul. He was the mightiest of men. God chose the only man that could have done what Paul did. What a warrior! I have been on the journeys of Paul from Israel through Syria, Turkey, Greece and Italy, which included the seven churches of the book of revelation. Next to Jesus as God and man, Paul was the greatest man of all history.

MISSION TRIP TO INDIA – 2015

The mission of this trip was to encourage the believers, to have four pastor conferences, to have two conferences for young people, which included college students, to distribute Bibles and distribute food, to minister to a group of widows and to preach in the local churches. But, most of all, our mission was to share the saving knowledge of Jesus Christ for salvation.

Pastors' Conferences – Approximately 200 pastors from all over India attended. We shared a lot. During the conferences, 25 prayed to receive Christ. This time was rich in God's blessings.

Youth and College Student Conferences – Wow! What great conferences. Maybe 100 students prayed to receive Christ. Boy, were they excited about that. Also ended up having many prayer meetings with the students. This time was very rich with God's blessings.

The Widows – There was a group of widows we ministered to. Most were old and in poor health. Body pain was with them from the time they woke up to the time they went to bed. They were extremely poor in worldly wealth. They were so thankful for the love shown to them by their pastor and this conference. Several prayed to receive Christ as their Savior. They were encouraged to know that someday their body pain will end and they will spend eternity in glory with the Lord.

Distribution of Bibles – 1000 bibles were purchased and distributed to everybody that we talked to. We visited orphanages and also attended a conference of widows. Quite a few of the widows prayed to receive Christ. Everybody we visited got a bible. It is my mission to make sure that everybody has the Word of God. Those that received the bibles were so grateful.

Distribution of Food – We also distributed food. The widows, the orphans, the pastors and the students all received meals. That, too, was important to me. You hear the expression "Nobody cares how much you know until they know how much you care". I wish you could have been there to feel the gratitude of those widows when we fed them and loved them.

Preached in Local Churches – Another wow! Was able to share how much God loves them. They knew that love of God. They spent much of their worship time on their knees with their hands raised to God, thanking Him and praising Him for all that He has done. It caused me to have tears in my eyes to watch them worship with such gratitude. By the way, they had no shoes and the church had no chairs. The floor was bare, and they sat on this hard floor for hours, and, yes, they were grateful for that hard floor – no complaining.

Salvations – There were a lot of salvations. Just think about that! Those that gave their lives to Christ will not suffer the consequences of hell. Praise and glory be to our God!

Summary – The people we met were, generally, downright good people with a good attitude. They live in total poverty by our standard. The pastor's house was 2 rooms total. They lived and slept in the same room. That room was maybe 20 feet by 20 feet. The other room was for storage and cooking. The kitchen had one small propane cooking stove. There was no refrigerator or anything else. The toilet was a small rectangular hole in the ground outside the two-room house. The pastor, his wife and two young adults lived in the house. They had one small two-wheel motorcycle that they all rode on to go to and from Church. They all squeezed together on that small motor-cycle. The pastor served his people 24 hours a day for seven days a week. The wife and the kids also served the Lord. They eat rice for breakfast, lunch and dinner. They had so little in comfort, but gave so much to others. With so little, they had so much joy and happiness. They lived the promise of Jesus – give, forgive, show mercy and you will find joy and happiness.

I found the people of India to be a wonderful people. They have so little and yet they are so grateful for what they do have. They worship Jesus with such gratitude that is not often seen here in our country with so much abundance.

Conclusion: Thank you, Lord for allowing me to experience this time with your people who would be called the "least of these" by worldly standards.

MISSION TRIP TO NEPAL
11/7/12 – 11/17/12

Agenda – Flew from Dallas to Dubai in the United Arab Emirates. Flew from Dubai to Kathmandu in Nepal. Drove 7 hours up to the top of the world in the Himalaya Mountain ranges to a place called Charikot. Charikot was our base of operations. We met our Nepal team members there. When we got to Charikot, it was like we stepped into a different world. It IS a different world; it is the top of the world. We also met the most wonderful people in the world – the Nepal brothers and sisters.

Each U.S. team member was given a local Nepal team member who was our translator. Also, a local church member was given to the U.S. and Nepal translator. These three made up a team that would canvas the countryside and hillsides to spread the saving knowledge of Jesus Christ. Other team members had a different objective and goal. They did not canvas the countryside but dedicated themselves to various local schools and orphanages to minister to the kids of these orphanages and schools and their parents. They also shared the saving knowledge of Jesus Christ. All of the U.S. members and the Nepal members blended together to form one big team to share one common goal: Show the love of Jesus and the saving grace of Jesus. It was amazing how this unified team loved one another and shared in the power of Jesus Christ. It felt like Jesus was there with us, and I am sure he was. Each morning a bus and two jeeps would take us to our various station points and drop us off. Some went to the schools and orphanages, and the rest of us to the hills, valleys and slopes. Sharing the gospel was very well-accepted and there were many salvations. We did, however, have to occasionally deal with the presence of Hinduism and Buddhism.

The Team Members – It is amazing how God called together a team of such diverse talents, temperaments, special skills and physical attributes. As I recall, we all worked together harmoniously to complete the total ministry, as Paul described the total ministry of Jesus by comparing it to the human body. Some must be like an eye and some like the nose and some like an ear. Which is more important to the whole body? None is more important. We are all equally important. I grew to love each member of the team. I also grew to love each member of the Nepal team. That love runs pretty deep.

Some Adventures – When we left Kathmandu, we traveled seven hours up to the top of the earth. To get there, we traveled gravel roads that were carved out of the hillsides. The roads were not much wider than the bus in most places. If the bus slid off the gravel road, it would have not stopped falling for a long time.

Actually, we had two fun experiences. In one instance, the bus came too close to the edge of the road and got stuck. Everybody got out of the bus, and we literally rebuilt the road.

In that process, the ground gave out from beneath me and I slid down the slope. Boy, was that exciting and fun! The second instance was when the bus had to make a very sharp turn on the edge of the cliff as we were going down a hill. The bus could not make the turn, and we were going down a very steep hill. Gravity was pulling the bus down the hill, but when the driver got the bus stopped, the front tire was within a foot of going over the edge. Everybody got out of the bus. The bus got stuck for a little bit as the driver tried to back up to adjust for the turn. The bus finally made the turn, but in this process, we were a foot away from meeting our Maker. Boy, was that fun and exciting!

Another experience for me and others was special and exciting. To reach the people who lived on the edge of a cliff and the slopes, we walked very narrow paths on the edge of slopes and cliffs. Of all the places I have been in this world, I have never been able to experience the way these beautiful people live their lives.

One more meaningful experience: One day I came upon a school where our team was working with the kids. It was unbelievable to see how they had the kids involved. The kids were getting it. This impact on the kids and parents was huge and will go on in their lives for their lifetime. I also watched the parents being involved by watching the kids. The parents were smiling. Thanks to the team for your work there. By the way, many kids accepted Jesus as their savior.

The Mission Coordinators and Missions Results – I know all of the members would want to thank the mission leaders, and God knows their names. They did an outstanding job. If anyone would desire to go on a mission trip, I would endorse the "East/West Ministries".

THE RESULTS:

Only God knows the total impact of the mission work done on this trip. The impact runs very deep from the members to the incidental acquaintances, the Nepal brothers and sisters and the direct and indirect people being ministered to. Thank you, Jesus, for this opportunity.

THE NUMBERS

Community Team: 910 heard the Gospel
218 indicated decisions for Christ
234 who were "seeking" received Bibles
Children's Team: 1,015 heard the Gospel
244+ indicated decisions for Christ
50 who were "seeking" received Bibles
TOTAL: 1,925 heard the Gospel
462+ indicated decisions for Christ
284 who were "seeking" received Bibles

Would I do it again? Yes! When is the next plane leaving? My suitcase is already packed!

MISSION TRIP TO THE PHILIPPINES – 2014

When Jesus came, He brought with Him a new dispensation. In the old covenant, God conquered by might, power and war. Jesus brought the new covenant which was to conquer by love, mercy and peace. (In fact, that is why the Jews missed Jesus as the long-awaited Messiah. They expected the Messiah to be a God who would conquer by might, war and force. Because of that, they missed the greatest blessing that God offered to man. What a shame.)

When Jesus brought the new covenant, He also brought the Holy Spirit. That Holy Spirit (God Himself) will dwell within those He has called to be the elect. Now, because of the Holy Spirit, God can work on a personal basis with each of his elect. Not only that, but because of the Holy Spirit, we have a spirit bond between all others who have the Holy Spirit. (An interesting point: The Holy Spirit does not have a limited dimension. The Holy Spirit can come and go when and where ever He chooses). This is so neat, so wonderful and powerful. That is why, I believe, a Spirit-filled person can feel the joy and sorrow of another Spirit-filled person. The indwelling of the Holy Spirit is also how a Spirit-filled person can feel the passion of God/ Jesus and His calling to do His will. This is also how a Spirit-filled person can feel the joy, pain and misery of another person halfway around the world.

Over the years, God has called me, through His Spirit, to go and help provide hope, mercy, love and and hands-on service to His people, even to all parts of the world I feel hope, mercy, love and hands-on service to His people, even to all parts of the world. I feel, actually I know, He is calling me to the Philippines again.. I can feel the agony and misery of the hurricane ravaged people Philippines. I must go!!!

TRIP TO TURKEY - 2010

My wife and I went on a two-week journey in the country of Turkey that ended up covering 2,000 miles through the southwestern and western portions of Turkey My primary goal was to retrace the footsteps of the Ambassador Paul, who wrote 2/3 of the New Testament under God's inspiration. We also visited the seven cities of the churches revealed to John in the book of Revelations. All I can say is WOW! WHAT AN EXPERIENCE! This journey allowed me the opportunity to feel and experience a little bit of the "Man behind the Man" – Paul. I had no idea what a powerful and driven man Paul was. God carefully chose the right man, and maybe the only man, to do what he did. After experiencing this journey, it is easy to see why God chose Paul.

The cities of that time were huge and extremely advanced in their technology. I cannot imagine how they were able to carve stone and erect those huge and beautiful stones in the form of buildings, archways, roads and palaces throughout the entire cities. These cities could accommodate 35,000 to 200,000 people. It would be difficult for modern technology and equipment to do the same. Incredible! The Roman roads were roads perfectly made out of large, hand-cut and hand-shaped rock that were approximately 3 feet by 3 feet by 2 feet deep. These roads extended for hundreds and hundreds of miles. The aqueducts, which were made of stone, extended for hundreds of miles. I was told that the slope on these aqueducts needed to be near perfect for the water to be carried for long distances. These structures were built over very steep mountain tops and on the sides of mountains. I saw very little, to none, flat terrains, so the Romans had to work with the topography they had. My eyes and mind could barely take it all in.

Now, back to the "Man behind the Man" – Paul. After experiencing this journey, I reread the book of Acts and Paul's letters to the churches that were established. The book of Acts and Paul's letters became alive. It was no longer a historical accounting of Paul's life and his calling by God to his appointed purpose, but it was kind of like experiencing his journey with him. It was almost like I could feel his passion for his mission and for the people he was ministering to. As an example, Luke, the author of the book of Acts, would convey an extremely difficult event in one single sentence. Luke would write that Paul went from one city to another city and not detail what the process entailed. To get from one point to another may have required him to travel 50, 75, 100 or more miles by foot through incredible, forbidding and radical terrain. Question: How did he do it? Also, look at all of the accounts that detail how he was beaten, and in one event left for dead and yet he tenaciously pursued God's will. He would go from one city of 50,000 to 200,000 people to another and confront the religious leaders about Jesus as the Christ. He would debate 20 or 30 religious leaders without fear. Paul was a man called by God and encouraged by God and enlightened by God to do what only Paul could have done. The "Man behind the Man" – Paul – was incredible and, next to Jesus, was the rock and cornerstone of what God wanted to reveal to His people about the last and only truth given to man. After three trips to Israel, a trip to Greece and this trip to Turkey, I will never be able to read the Bible the same way I used to read it. The Bible is alive and is the living Word of God.

What I have learned through these experiences is this: The world we live in is a sinful, self-serving and self-destructing world that will drive itself into the pits of hell. God has offered us a way out of hell, but it requires self denial and a heart for serving a fair and just God. To serve God will require us to be separated from the world and its evilness. To serve God will require obedience to His Word, self denial and hardships. In the Garden of Gethsemane, Jesus said, "Let Thy will be done", and those words caused him to suffer a death on the cross of His earthly flesh. Paul also said, "Let Thy will be done," and it cost him all of life's comforts and ultimately his life. The thing I like about Paul is this: He said, "I rejoice in all things to serve the Lord, and especially in my suffering for the cause of Jesus Christ". The big question is this: Will we say, "Let Thy will be done", or will we say "Let my will be done"? God knows the difference. At judgment, He will know and we will be accountable, and then there is the judgment.

While in Turkey, I was able to approach the people, mostly young people, about eternal security. As you know, Turkey is primarily Muslim. They had no knowledge of how to get into heaven. Their religion is works based and offers no assurance of going to their heaven, with one exception. That exception is to commit Jihad in the name of Allah. I talked to them about how God sent Jesus to die and provide a way into heaven. THEY WERE MORE THAN INTERESTED. So, I asked them how they became a Muslim, and they said because their father and mother were Muslim. They went on to say they did not know much about the principals of being a Muslim. They also said they were fearful to change from being a Muslim

I think a lot of these people are ready for the good news of Jesus Christ. By the way, the Turkish people are not descendents of Ishmael (Arabic). They are primarily Mongolian, so they do not have the curse given to the descendants of Ishmael. We, the Christians, need to get outside of the church walls and go to work. The world is ready.

CPSIA information can be obtained at www.ICGtesting.com
Printed in the USA
LVOW06s1510040915

452608LV00016B/132/P